D0938557

The 30,000-Mile Ski Race

The 30,000-Mile

1972

Ski Race

Peter Miller

The Dial Press · New York

Library of Congress Calaloging in Publication Data
Miller, Peter, 1934–
   The 30,000-mile ski race.
      1.   Ski racing.   I.   Title.
GV854.9.R3M5   796.9'3   74–37438

Library of Congress Catalog Card Number: 74–37438

Printed in the United States of America

First Printing
Designed by The Etheredges

In memory of Ross Milne,
Australian National Ski Team, killed on the Patscherkofel
downhill at Innsbruck, Austria, January 30, 1964;
Michel Bozon,
French National Ski Team, killed on the
Emile Allais downhill at Mégève, France, January 23, 1970;
and of Barbi Hennenberger,
German National Ski Team, and
Bud Werner,
American National Ski Team, killed in an avalanche
at St.-Moritz, Switzerland, April 23, 1964

Contents

Foreword

In ski racing, as in other sports, there is much more to competition than simple results. In my quest for a gold medal, my desire to be best, the results were extremely important, but equally significant were the who and why of what happened.

Certainly, it is true that the results sheet can offer us clues about ski racers. Are they consistent or just lucky (or unlucky)? Are they persistent or do they give up too easily? Are they good under pressure? Strong? But the real and interesting story of the racers lies beyond these clues. What are the racers really like? What is their background, motivation and personality? How do they react to the sport? How do the results affect them?

In *The 30,000-Mile Ski Race*, Peter Miller goes behind the scoreboard and answers these questions for us. Racers like Tyler Palmer, Rick Chaffee and Marilyn Cochran become more than names on the results sheet and ski racing becomes more than just sliding down the mountain as fast as you can go.

This is a book which recognizes the reality that the international race circuit is not all glamor and excitement. You might think this is what it's like for racers traveling from one glamorous resort to another. But ski racing for much of the time is hard work and drudgery. Peter Miller accurately captures the reality of the hard times as well as the high moments.

Written as it is from an American point of view, *The 30,000-Mile Ski Race* has a lot to say about the U.S. Ski Team of which I was a member for eight years. It reveals the worry over money which affects many of our young American racers. In my opinion, the kids on the U.S. Ski Team are being hypocritical and short-sighted in their recurring complaints about not making any money while ski racing. On the one hand—employing the rhetoric of today's youth—they criticize and condemn money and material possessions; on the other hand, they are quick to blame lack of money for their "not doing well in racing." This is bitching of the most inconsistent sort.

Failure to recognize this hypocrisy in the kids—to expose it and replace it with something positive—is the fault of the coaches. They should aim at replacing the racers' sense of being valueless with more constructive goals. A good coaching program should recognize this opportunity and concentrate on the mental aspects of ski racing. An approach to breaking down the mental barriers to winning would do as much as all the physical training and technique analyses that are now heaped upon the U.S. Ski Team. Yet, year after year, we fail to take the mental considerations of the racer into account.

The 30,000-Mile Ski Race shows clearly that for a European skier, winning the World Cup or an Olympic medal is a sure path to wealth and to raising himself from obscurity. For the European, it is the way to assert his individuality and independence. Too often, for the young American racer, "asserting your individuality and independence" is to wear your hair long, leave your shirttails out and ski in bedraggled levis. I find this approach ridiculous. If you're serious about ski racing, the way to individuality and independence quite simply is by winning races. Perhaps we have to relearn that fundamental truth. The hard fact of the matter is that every winter in the World Cup, only two people, a boy and a girl, are the world's best skiers, and every second year there are only a half dozen gold medal winners.

Peter Miller's book addresses itself to the problem: How do you discipline the U.S. Ski Team? By imposing the will of the coaches? Or by getting the racers to learn self-discipline? Perhaps the clearest answer was given in the winter of 1971 by Spider Sabich. Failing miserably on the World Cup circuit and not responding to the strict discipline of the U.S. Ski Team, Sabich left Europe to join the pro circuit in America. Here, a racer is strictly on his own. What he accomplishes is in and of his own doing and self-discipline. Sabich immediately responded by winning his first pro race and going on to become the winter's top money winner.

The lesson of Sabich is that self-discipline is the key to winning ski races, and the job of coaching, rather than yelling at "unruly" kids and constantly pointing out their faults, is to provide an environment in which the racers can learn once and for all that their success depends on disciplining themselves. Often this simply means that a racer have the chance to sit back and think about his problems rather than haul himself to the top to take another run through the flags. And if a racer is incapable of disciplining himself, he doesn't belong on the team.

It is a credit to Peter Miller and to his book that this problem of the U.S. Ski Team surfaces in such a credible way that we may never be able to ignore it again.

—BILLY KIDD

1964 Olympic silver medalist
1970 Combined gold medal winner in
*   the FIS World Ski Championships*
1970 Pro Skier of the Year
Racing Editor, SKI Magazine

Preface

Ski racing is unique. It is a dangerous, lonely sport, where each individual is racing against the clock and himself. It is a technical sport that demands precision and split-second reactions that are developed over years of training and constant practice; a ski racer can lose his timing after three weeks of being off his skis. It is most similar to grand prix auto racing.

This book began as a simple journalistic look at the highest level of international ski competition—the World Cup. But an undercurrent emerged that I believe mirrors our society and delineates how our customs have shaped the young American. Perhaps it stems from the fact that the Americans are competing against Europeans in Europe, and the American men are usually losing. They are often broke and they are confused about their ambitions and goals. The American racer is the product of a supposedly superior society that has been first in business, science, efficiency, war and sports. He has been raised in the mountain areas of our country, within a society that is 90 percent white. His family may be comparatively poor, but there is always money for ski equipment, ski lift tickets and cars. The American racer expects to go to college, to have a good job, and to live well. He likes to think for himself, and he does not like discipline nor regimentation.

The European mountain youth, on the other hand, does not expect to go to college, does not expect to have a good job, but does expect to work hard. For him, ski racing is a college diploma. If he graduates with honor —comes in first—he will have a career and live a better life. Ski racing can give him pride, for he may become a national hero. He will travel to places he would never have visited. His position on the national ski team of his country is a status symbol. He is envied by fellow skiers and the public.

The American looks upon ski racing as a phase of life. Sometimes he is racing because his parents, surrogate competitors, want him to. Most American skiers do not have the ambition or discipline to train eight months a year for five years and then perhaps find they do not have what it takes to win an international ski race.

The American racer has never felt at ease in Europe. There is a psychological barrier to crack, for he is competing in the opposition's front parlor. For some reason many Americans develop an inferiority complex when they cross the Atlantic. Perhaps they feel they do not have the cultural background, that they will make fools of themselves, because they cannot speak the language. During the 1970–71 season, the American Ski Team traveled 30,000 miles during the World Cup circuit, not including a side trip to Japan made by the coach and a few of the racers. From the first week in December until the middle of March they raced in nine countries. It was a formidable itinerary:

MEN		WOMEN	
11 December.	*Sestriere, Italy*	12 December.	*Sestriere, Italy*
16 December.	*Val d'Isère, France*	17 December.	*Val d'Isère, France*
5 January.	*Berchtesgaden, W. Germany*	4 January.	*Maribor, Yugoslavia*
		8 January.	*Oberstaufen, W. Germany*

9 January.	*Madonna di Campiglio, Italy*	12 January.	*Grindelwald, Switzerland*
16 January.	*St.-Moritz, Switzerland*	19 January.	*Schruns, Austria*
18 January.	*Adelboden, Switzerland*	28 January.	*Pra-Loup, France*
19 January.	*Badgastein, Austria*	29 January.	*St.-Gervais, France*
24 January.	*Kitzbühel, Austria*	5 February.	*Mürren, Switzerland*
31 January.	*Mégève, France*	13 February.	*Mont Ste.-Anne, Quebec, Canada*
5 February.	*Crans-Montana, Switzerland*	19 February.	*Sugarloaf, Maine*
7 February.	*Mürren, Switzerland*	27 February.	*Heavenly Valley, California*
14 February.	*Mont Ste.-Anne, Quebec, Canada*	10 March.	*Abetone, Italy*
19 February.	*Sugarloaf, Maine*	14 March.	*Åre, Sweden*
28 February.	*Heavenly Valley, California*		
14 March.	*Åre, Sweden*		

For most of this schedule there were no hamburgers, little of their favorite music, no lounging about with their friends, no movies. There was little news from home, because their mail rarely caught up with them. They received little publicity from the American press and the publicity they did receive was often critical. And then there were planes and trains to catch, schedules to meet.

Perhaps the American male's poor record in ski racing is the result of a combination of factors that is best expressed in the phrase "he can't put it all together." It might also have something to do with coaches. The American system is to give a racer a time trial. If he does well, he is on the team. If he does poorly, he is off. This black and white approach neglects the character of a young athlete who may not do well in a time trial but has a most glittering talent that could be brought out through physical training, development of particular skills and a very careful use of psychology. Europeans, particularly the French, seem, at times, to be much more aware of the human element in the ski racer; an athlete can be a very sensitive person.

The American ski racer is an enigma to the Europeans. They see flashes of brilliance in a few competitors, then nothing. Many Americans cannot answer why the American male racer continues to be fourth-rate. The young American is a complex, introspective creature. He is not sure what he expects, for he has many goals. He is on a multiple quest, and sometimes he loses sight of the fact that in international competition, most racers compete, very simply, to win.

What is it about skiing? The sport grabs your body and psyche and never lets go. Mine was seduced at the age of six and I am still under the influence. It is one of the reasons why my family moved to Vermont when I was a youngster. It is why I quit a New York job with a very promising future; I wanted to be on the slopes and to live near them. Most of my friendships have developed because of a mutual attachment to the sport. In a way, I am indebted to all of these friends, for this book is the result of longtime, sustained enthusiasm and curiosity about skiing.

A number of friends helped me with this book. John Fry is the editor in chief of *Ski* Magazine, and, over a few beers in Stowe, Vermont, he suggested the idea, put me in touch with a book publisher and sent me on my way to Europe for six months. Del Mulkey is an old ski pal who lives in Paris and photographs the ski scene all over the world. Some of his photographs are in this book. He is a good photographer, but a better friend. Del introduced me to Harvey Edwards, a journalist who lives in Chamonix and who did the research on the Europeans. Through our many conversations he gave me a thorough briefing on what ski racing means to the European. He is an easy man to travel with, the only one I know who could find a charming pension in Kitzbühel for $3.00 a night, with a view of the slalom course and a pasture with a pile of manure in it. Every morning a farmer pushed wheelbarrow loads from the barn to the pile and, in the background, the racers would be climbing the slalom hill.

Robert Blanc is the director of Les Arcs resort near Bourg-St.-Maurice, France. He is a superb skier and mountain guide and a new friend. He was kind enough to lend me the use of an apartment so I could write this book in peace. Barbara Severit also worked at Les Arcs. Barbara answered my correspondence, typed my manuscripts and filled in a lot of those little facts that are difficult to verify. She is a good companion, a good listener and a good skier.

I want to thank the American Ski Team, and their coach Willy Schaeffler. He and the team put up with me and my little tape recorder, and it was good of them. It was also good of Air France and S.A.S. to arrange transportation for me to Paris and Stockholm. Both airlines specialize in super food and service.

I also apologize to two fine and beautiful young skiers, Dods and Hilary Miller, who did not have a chance to ski all winter with their Dad.

And finally I wish to acknowledge the SOBs that stole two pairs of ski poles from me. May a thousand camel ants . . .

PETER MILLER

Les Arcs, France

June 1971

In this country
you either finish first or last,
there is no second place.
—BUDDY WERNER

The 30,000-Mile Ski Race

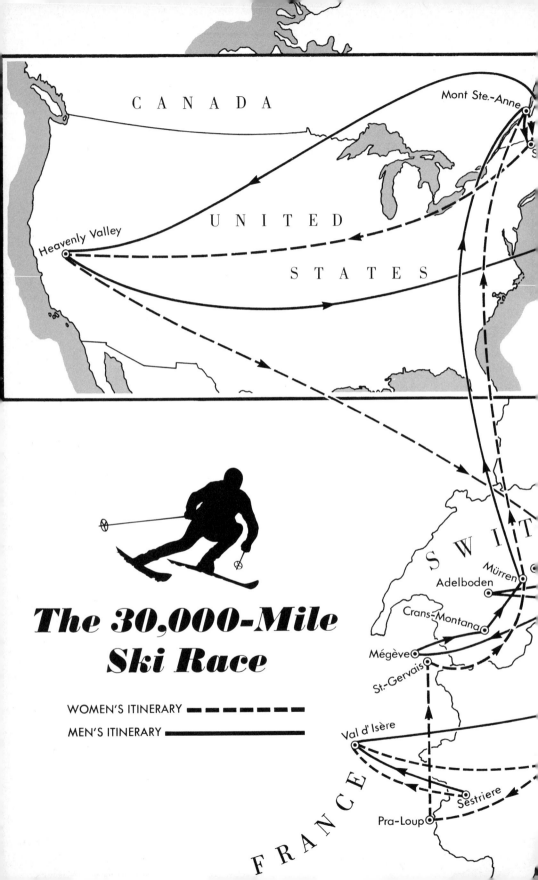

The 30,000-Mile Ski Race

WOMEN'S ITINERARY ▬ ▬ ▬ ▬

MEN'S ITINERARY ▬▬▬▬▬▬

CANADA

Mont Ste.-Anne

UNITED

STATES

Heavenly Valley

S W I T

Mürren

Adelboden

Crans-Montana

Mégève

St.-Gervais

Val d'Isère

Sestriere

Pra-Loup

F R A N C E

NORWAY

SWEDEN

Åre

WEST

GERMANY

Oberstaufen

Kitzbühel

Berchtesgaden

Schruns

A U S T R I A

Badgastein

d

St.-Moritz

Maribor

Madonna di Campiglio

I T A L Y

YUGOSLAVIA

Abetone

The Etheredges

The trophy stands eighteen inches tall, fifteen pounds of crystal molded into a globe that rests on a pedestal. Longitudinal and latitudinal lines and small prismatic circles are cut onto the face of the crystal. It is the World Cup. One each of these trophies is given annually to the best female and male skiers in the world, or at least to those who have competed in sanctioned World Cup races and who have earned the highest number of points computed on their best finishes in downhill, slalom and giant slalom events. The World Cup is the most desired trophy for the ski competitor, for the ski equipment manufacturer and for ski-oriented countries.

If you look into the trophy at the right angle, the small etched circles will reflect your face in dozens of tiny vignettes—a narcissistic mirror. Jean-Claude Killy of France has gazed deeply into the two World Cups he has won, and he has profited greatly. So has Karl Schranz of Austria, who

1. The Cup

also won two cups. During the '70–'71 season, Gustavo Thoeni, a twenty-year-old Italian from a small hill town, skied fluidly and with genius. Now he owns a cup and is on his way to wealth. The cup is magic.

Magic? Each cup produced costs $2,000. Total expenses for promotion of the World Cup are about $400,000 per year, which is quite a bit more than is earned by the skiers who win it. Evian picks up the tab. Evian is especially good to drink before skiing, during skiing, and after skiing. It is good with meals, for old age, and after making love. Evian is good for everything. It should be; it is water that, according to the proprietors, is extracted from the glaciers of Mont Blanc. The official name of the World Cup is Coupe du Monde de Ski, F.I.S., trophée Evian.

The World Cup (trophée Evian) is a very good business arrangement. There are two circuits for the World Cup, one for men and one for women.

The $2,000 World Cup.

Over the winter of '70–'71 the racers, competing as national teams, entered forty-seven races at twenty-one ski resorts in nine countries in Europe and North America. They traveled over 30,000 miles by train, plane, bus and car. There are about one hundred hard-core competitors on the two circuits, and they are accompanied by coaches, trainers, technicians, officials and a rabble of other racer chasers, including about fifty journalists.

Transportation companies benefit. The European resorts fight to sponsor a World Cup race, because the journalists will give them worldwide publicity. Television doubles publicity (in Europe the races are shown live) and defrays expenses. Most resorts consider the $30,000 to $40,000 spent preparing for a World Cup event a fine publicity investment. So do liquor, cigarette, food and hot drink companies. Longines and Omega time the races and the two companies spend up to $500,000 each year on equipment and personnel. All these companies are deeply involved in advertising the dictum, "What's good for healthy, sane ski racers is good for you!"

The ski racers? Sometimes they win and become famous and wealthy. Usually, though, they lose. Sometimes they are injured and are forced to retire from competition. There is the chance of death from a high-speed crash. Ski racers are highly developed and trained animals who, so to speak, are tools of the trade. In European Alpine countries, winning national skiers not only afford pride to their fellow citizens; they, through publicity, raise the number of ski tourists who visit their resorts. So ski racing is promoted by the government. It helps defray expenses of the team, and in some countries elite skiers are welcomed into the customs service, which pays them a monthly salary of $150 and up.

The ski racer is also, in a way, a test pilot and a model. Manufacturers supply the racers with skis and boots, which the racers test and improve. They are also equipped with ski poles, racing suits, sweaters, parkas, goggles, helmets and hats, skin cream—even, on occasion, cars. For this right, the manufacturers pay either the skier or the skier's national ski federation which, according to its morality, may or may not in turn pay the ski racers. Karl Schranz and Gustavo Thoeni make about $50,000 per year according to some questionable rumors. The Swiss Ski Federation pays the racers and makes savings deposits for them—they can only draw upon the latter after they have retired from competition. Although there is tremendous revenue to be reaped from ski competition, the ski racer is not supposed to profit. He is an amateur (so he can qualify for the Olympics) who theoretically races for the pleasure of the sport. He should train and race eight or nine months a year, blast out of the starting gate, go like hell, and if he crashes and breaks his back, well, that is his luck.

In Europe, ski racing is a profession. The dream of many Alpine village youngsters is to be on the national ski team, to win, travel, be a sports hero and in later life own a small hotel. Ski racing is the only way out, or up, from the life of simplicity, which so many Americans, drowning in material success, are now trying to achieve. These young Europeans work hard to race and to win. They are very mature at an early age and direct their energy in total devotion to their goal. They want to win, to be recognized. Heroes are still a legitimate commodity in Europe, to be idolized and respected, and if their goal is to win the World Cup, they remain content to have this goal imprison their minds, bodies, and lives. These young European ski racers hope that they may become another Killy, Schranz, or Thoeni. It is not probable, but it is possible.

On the other hand, the American racers are completely amateur. By rule of the United States Ski Association, there is to be no compensation to the racer, no payment for racing on specified ski products (although the ski equipment manufacturers in 1970 paid $80,000 to the U.S.S.A. for the American national team to compete, for one year, on their products), no financial compensation at all.

Ski racers are race horses—except that the odds are a little higher with the horses to win, show or place—and American racers receive about the same treatment as do the horses that are whipped around a race track: food, a place to sleep, medical treatment, and transportation. Unlike a horse, the male American racer has personal financial problems. He is anxious about the draft, about trying to race while obtaining a college education. At the back of his mind, hidden in his subconscious, which he is trying to program to lift himself into the winner's circle, is that fear of the future: what happens after? The female American racers, who have few of these problems, do much better in the international circuit. Ski racing is not an honorable profession in the United States, and when a racer who usually wins in the States ends sixtieth in his first international ski race, well, his psyche gets bruised. He begins to think he is a bum. It is a long way to the top, and those Americans who finish within the top fifteen believe they have overcome far more than the Europeans, who have been trained to function as efficiently as an integrated circuit in an Omega timing unit. The American racer is a lonely figure on the international circuit. He is an amateur competing against professionals.

Still, the American racers break through every so often: Buddy Werner, who was injured more often than he won, and died in an avalanche; Billy Kidd, a brilliant competitor who was also injury prone; Jim Heuga, a gifted skier who never attained his potential. Now there is another American developing into a ski star, Tyler Palmer, a New Hampshire boy, who traveled the European circuit for the first time in '69–'70.

Tyler has a strong desire to compete against adversity and to come out on top. He disdains the organization, smolders because he is not allowed to make money while he races. Then he shrugs his shoulders and says, "Screw them! It'll come someday." Tyler is the exception to the American syndrome of mediocrity in ski racing.

The European super skiers are glittering stars. The Americans and a few other outsiders follow the World Cup in the hope that their star may also glitter, however briefly. The '70–'71 season started early for international ski racers. For the European teams—the French, Austrian, Swiss and Italians—training began the first week in July with calisthenics and physical conditioning, sometimes at the seaside, but usually in the mountains on a glacier. They played tennis, bicycled, ran up and down mountains, went through exercises specifically designed to strengthen the ski muscles—legs, stomach, shoulders—and to develop their sense of balance. They skied on the glaciers, practicing downhill and slalom. By the beginning of the race season in December, the French ski team had run three hundred miles of downhill and skied through 15,000 slalom gates. During the summer some raced in Australia and Chile.

By contrast, the American team's training was haphazard. Some of the team members had attended summer school, others worked, hoping to save enough money so they could race during the winter. They had a two-week training camp during the summer in California. Some of the better racers were sent to Australia to compete and practice for a few weeks. In October the women and men attended another training camp for a week and then practiced for the month of November. By December, when the international racing season began, they had less than half the amount of training that the Europeans had received during the summer and fall. They had a lot of catching up to do.

It was a bright day, warm in the sun, and on the terraces in the center of Val d'Isère indolent skiers and the other people who did not work during the day were absorbing the warmth into their bodies, hoping it would last into the night. From their seats they could gaze at the mountains that loom around the village. To the north the mountains were snow covered and laced with ski trails and lifts. To the south and east the sun had melted the snow from them and obscenely exposed their brown, shaley sides. Parapets were built into those mountains, and roads zig-zagged up their slopes, seeming, at first glance, to lead to a high-altitude mining operation. But the road and parapets acted as retainers to keep the town from being showered by avalanches.

On December 15 there was not enough snow to avalanche, just enough

2. The Crash

to ski on, and to race. Val d'Isère is France's most sportive ski resort, and a large troupe of racers, coaches, trainers and racer-chasers—ski equipment representatives, technicians, officials, public relationists, journalists, race fans, relatives, groupies and other hangers-on—had driven to the resort to race, to watch the race, to be watched, to make some money, to have fun.

Although the first race of the season had been in Sestriere, Italy, the traditional and unofficial opening of the World Cup ski racing and social scene was here in Val d'Isère. Here grouped the caravan that would travel throughout the winter sports spas of Europe and America, ostensibly to see who were the best racers in the world. The Val d'Isère event is known as the *Critérium International de la Première Neige* and *Coupe Henri Oreiller*. One reason for the excitement and anticipation is that the latter race, the *Coupe*

Henri, is held on one of the more exciting downhill trails in Europe, and nearly everybody likes to watch a skier going seventy miles per hour down a mountain and maybe obliterating himself in a crash.

Of the 208 racers and fifty-odd coaches and trainers on hand—representing sixteen countries, including Japan and Lichtenstein—twenty-four were American: three coaches, two managers, one doctor, nine girl racers, nine men, all traveling on a $40,000 budget from the United States Ski Association. On the afternoon of the fifteenth at the finish of the downhill, they lined up for a team photograph. The sun had just sunk behind the

The town of Val d'Isère.

Avalanche fences along the slopes
above the town.

summit of the Bellevarde, high over their heads, where the downhill trail begins. It had been a day of training on the downhill, as required by the rules, so that the racers would be familiar with the speed and dangers of the course. The training was finished for the day, and the Americans' thoughts had not yet turned to tomorrow's program—a slalom race for the girls, more downhill training for the men. They smiled easily for the photographer—a new team, new coaches, and forty-five races to go. New places to see and the excitement, perhaps, of victory. The racers came from similar backgrounds, raised within a middle-class society in small towns near the mountains and ski slopes; half were from the Rockies and the Sierras, half were from the Adirondacks, the Green and White Mountains of New England. Their parents had started them on their racing careers, driving them to the ski slopes, buying them tickets and equipping them with several hundred dollars' worth of skis, boots, poles and clothes. Most of the racers were attending college or had recently graduated. They were young, the girls averaging nineteen years, the men slightly under twenty-one.

At fifty-four, their head coach, Willy Schaeffler, was a good generation gap older. His hair is grey, thin and combed straight back, close to his skull. Part of his face seems to be paralyzed, so that his smile stops in the middle. Willy is a neat dresser and walks erect, almost stiffly. His blue eyes are appraising and sometimes appear quite cold. He spent the first half of his life in Germany, where he was born.

He had told the team earlier, when they were training in Aspen, Colorado, that he was the team hatchet man and that if someone had to be kicked off the team, he would do it, and he would be the scapegoat for all the difficulties. He had also told them that he was going to discipline their minds and bodies, and that although skiing is an individual sport, everyone must work together. And that meant schedules. He planned to run a tightly regimented organization. He wanted to develop winners.

Willy has been a winner all his life. In his twenty-two years as the coach at the University of Denver his ski teams won 100 out of 123 dual meets, and 14 National Collegiate titles. For a while, his arch rival was Bob Beattie, who, before he became one of Willy's predecessors as National Ski Team coach, trained the ski team at the University of Colorado. Willy beat the pants off Bob. Most of the team did not appreciate Willy's author-

Willy Schaeffler.

The American team at Val d'Isère. The women: Barbara Ann Cochran, Sandra Poulsen, Janet Turner, Susan Corrock, Patty Boydstun, Lindy Cochran, Penny Northrup, Marilyn Cochran, Karen Budge. The men: Tom Kelly (trainer), Willy Schaeffler, Hanspeter Rohr (assistant coach), Steve Lathrop, Bob Cochran, Craig Shanholtzer, Rogers Little, Rudd Pyles, Mike Lafferty, Hank Tauber (girls' coach), Eric Poulsen, Hank Kashiwa. Missing: Rick Chaffee, Tyler Palmer, Spider Sabich.

itarian attitude toward ski racing. Willy smiled tightly at the photographer.

Standing next to him for the picture was his assistant coach, Hanspeter Rohr. He is twenty-six, and it was his first season as a coach. During the '69–'70 season, he was one of Switzerland's top downhillers until, in the Wengen, Switzerland, downhill, he crashed at seventy miles per hour and left a large splotch of blood on the snow, tore the ligaments in his left foot and leg, bent in the ankle bone, broke the right leg, dislocated his shoulder, broke his nose, injured his eye, scraped the skin off half of his face and tore the back shoulder muscle. Four operations later he decided his racing career was over. He hoped to make the Americans into good downhillers.

The women's coach, Hank Tauber, twenty-nine, wanted to pull the girls into the winning circle, and he also believed the route lay with regimentation. He had top racers in two sisters from Vermont, Marilyn and Barbara Ann Cochran, but the rest had to be trained and pushed.

The American ski racers had been tested psychologically, and the tests showed that they valued their independence highly. The tests also pointed out that the downhill racers were tense, assertive and evaded rules. Craig Shanholtzer was a downhill specialist, and it was his first year on the circuit—the rookie. Bob Cochran was ranked thirteenth in the world in downhill and wanted to win a World Cup race. Hank Kashiwa, a three-year veteran, hoped to sort out things in his head and win a medal in the

Hank Tauber, women's coach, tapes number to Janet Turner's back.

Racer in training on the upper part of the Val d'Isère downhill course.

Olympics. He was developing downhill skills. Spider Sabich, who missed the picture session—he was off doing something else—preferred slalom. These young racers, and the rest of the team—there were no heroes among them, no super athletes—hoped to match the vast superiority of the French, Austrian, Italian and Swiss skiers. Well, maybe in one race.

The team picture was taken at 1/250th of a second, slightly less time than it took Rudd Pyles, a quiet Coloradoan who is a talented downhiller, to relax his face into an easy smile. A ski racer can win or lose in the time it takes to smile. In a downhill it takes just a little longer to crash and possibly smash your body to bits. No one thought about that. It was time to load into the Peugeot bus and head back to the Hotel Val d'Isère, shuck off the ski clothes, take a bath or sauna, and then go to the local pastry shop for something sweet, talk with racers from other national teams, perhaps make a new friend. Time is short for a ski racer during the season—a few hours in the afternoon after a day on the hill, then dinner at seven thirty, and to bed early.

Rudd Pyles is a six-footer, strongly built. His face is thick, heavy in the cheeks and jowls, but handsome in the American way—square-faced, long, full lips, a strong chin and well-proportioned nose. His grey-green eyes look directly into you, easily, and he blinks in a slow, measured cadence. He is a quiet person and chooses his words with care; no one could ever be flippant with Rudd. He would have been the team leader if there was such a thing; he felt honored to be on the American Ski Team, and it bothered him to see team members acting up when parading in their uniforms. He works hard at ski racing, but he enjoys it immensely. He wants to win. In '69–'70, his first tour of Europe, he started sixty-sixth in his first downhill race at Val d'Isère. He placed sixth, and at the World Championships in Val Gardena he finished eleventh. Rudd was the American team's best prospect to win a World Cup race.

The day after the American team had its photograph taken, Rudd was one of ninety-eight racers in training on the OK downhill, named after Henri Oreiller and Jean-Claude Killy, two of the famous native sons who helped to make Val d'Isère known as the resort of champions. The day was as clear and bright as mountain water. Rudd and his teammates rode the red, blue and yellow gondolas of the Daille lift up above the timberline, past the mid-station, to the top of the Bellevarde. Each was to have another run down the course, and as they waited for their running number to be called, they soaked in the sun. There was little wind.

The starting gate was a wooden structure that looked as hastily put together as a new outhouse. During the race, sophisticated Longines timing equipment would measure to 1/100th of a second the time, from start to finish, of each racer. But in training, timing was in the hands of the team coaches and trainers, positioned at the start, halfway down the course, and

Finish of the downhill.

Start of the downhill.

at the finish. Each man was equipped with a stopwatch and a walkie-talkie to measure the halfway and finish times of their racers and then compare these times with the times of the previous day's training, and with the times of those racers favored to win. Somewhere on the course, usually at different turns, were other trainers with their eyes locked into small videotape cameras. In the evenings the tapes would be played so the racers could hopefully pick out some flaw in their style or in the line they raced. The American team had one video camera, the French three.

Downhillers are as carefully dressed as matadors, perhaps not with so many frills and with more common sense. The racers are zipped into one-piece suits, usually colorful and as tight as snake skin. They were first developed by the French. The suit cuts down wind resistance and so increases the speed of the racer. The original version had one zipper and the racers found it was impractical. Now the suit has an additional zipper—a four-inch horizontal affair at the crotch. A plastic helmet protects the head from wind, cold and serious injury. It has a psychological effect too.

Hank Kashiwa's downhill equipment.

Before racers were required to wear helmets, they wore wool caps. During the race the noise of the wind whistling into their ears because of high speed often caused fear. Now the helmets shut out the noise.

The American uniform is a sober two-tone blue, slightly iridescent. The helmet is red and blue and star speckled, as are the warm-up suits and sweaters. "This ski uniform, it is a scandal," yelped one of the French technicians. "Flags and stars on their shoulders, gloves, pants, helmets, maybe they have them on their underpants?" It is hard, in Europe, for an American to do anything right.

Rudd's mind was locked into the course. The previous day he had two fast runs that equaled the times of Henri Duvillard and Karl Cordin, France and Austria's two best downhillers, and he was confident. Four days earlier, at the season's first race in Sestriere, Italy, he had skied slowly in training, then gone all out in the race and crashed halfway down the course. "I really was a dumb bastard to go so fast," he commented to a friend, one of the few times he has been heard to swear. He had changed his technique for the Val d'Isère race—he was going all out in training, then would relax in the downhill. Rudd had not raced at over fifty-five miles per hour during a month of training in Aspen, Colorado, and he realized that his timing was not as sharp as it should have been. The French team had had 240 miles of downhill running since they went into training in July, and for ten days in early December they had been running the OK downhill. They were up for the race.

"Beep!" the trainers chirped into their radios and Karl Cordin, Austria's youngest new star, was on the course. "Beep!" and World Cup champion Karl Schranz poled out of the starting gate a minute later. Then Henri Duvillard and the crazy, happy Malcolm Milne of Australia. Each racer was testing the course, searching for the perfect line and the speed that would carry him faster than the day before. "Beep!" and Bob Cochran was off.

Rudd's bindings were set to release at 396 pounds, his 222-centimeter K2 skis, striped in red, white and blue, were waxed with Swix green and paraffin. A good combination, thought Rudd; he had confidence in the skis—they were in top shape. "Beep!" and he was out of the gate, poling, skating, then dropping his body into an egg-shaped crouch that would lessen the wind resistance, so his skis would slide faster. He hit the first steep dropoff and was riding his skis lightly at sixty miles per hour, following the ribbon of carefully manicured snow that ended more than two miles below in the valley. The downhill trail, about thirty yards wide, was lined on each side by small red and white Evian flags. Thirty-one control gates were set on the course, and it is running through these gates that the racer hopes to find the fastest line to the finish. If he cuts the corners well, his time should be slightly over two minutes.

Speed, speed, speed, this is what makes a downhiller. He must love speed, the feeling of conquering a mountain with his skis, his body, his mind. The top speed of a downhill racer has been measured at 82.5 miles per hour. Yet downhillers who rely only on speed do not last long. They must have other qualities, particularly the strength and suppleness of a thoroughly trained body that can control speed. They must have a sense of what they call in France *glissement*—the ability to slide their skis well. They must know how to relax their ankles and knees so that both skis ride flat on the snow, which gives them more speed. They must predict the difficulties of speed in relation to turns and bumps. Some of this knowledge is acquired but much of the downhiller's psyche is intuitive. And aggressive.

The psychological studies of the American racers supported the premise that the downhiller is an extrovert. This is not necessarily true; downhillers are usually lucid, calm individuals. They do not react with the quick movements of the slalom skier fighting for 1/100th of a second on many turns; the downhiller gains split seconds with a feeling of the whole race. Yet if he misses his line or slides a turn at a crucial point, he can blow the race. If he does not know his speed he may crash disastrously. The downhiller must always be on the edge between the highest speed and safety, riding the skis into the inner limits of danger. "You need guts to run downhill," said Karl Schranz, who was World Champion two years in a row, "and not everyone has it."

Rudd—you could call him an introvert—was thinking only of speed after he poled onto the course and crouched his body into the egg position. He limbered his knees and ankles, softening them so he could feel contact between his feet, the skis, and snow—a feeling of riding the skis flatly, efficiently. His eyes were on the first steep dropoff; he would press low into this pitch to pick up speed for the flat below.

No trees cover this portion of the downhill; it is rolling, snowcovered terrain of thousands of acres barren of people save the racers and trainers, and a few recreational skiers, an undulating white desert dominated by the

Rudd Pyles.

Grande Motte glacier. The racers glided through this scenery, as infinitesimal as the billions of snow crystals that compose the huge plateau.

The snow was soft and whispery, light and deep, but on the course it was packed very hard, almost icy. Very few bumps were in the trail; the snow was meticulously prepared for high speed. The upper part was smooth, flat and shiny. It sucked the speed out of Rudd and he could feel the exhilaration as he accelerated.

Rudd was always fast. At the age of five, he was racing on Chalk Mountain in the mining town of Climax, Colorado, on a slope his grandfather and a few friends spent seventy days clearing in 1932. Rudd's mother recalled that he was always the fastest among his friends, snowplowing straight down the hill. During the dry, cold evenings he, his brother and the others would strap on their skis and chase rabbits down the mountain, through the forests, and sometimes they would play tag or hide and seek, their yells and laughter muffled by the pines and fir trees. Moments like these Rudd recalls fondly and with amusement. His desire to ski fast grew with him, and he practiced as a young racer at nearby Arapahoe Basin, where Willy Schaeffler, now his coach, was the ski school director; Willy remembers Rudd at that time as having a head that looked like an overgrown pumpkin, his racing helmet was so big. Rudd's racing progressed

through a cracked ankle and two dislocated shoulders. He was named to the American Ski Team in 1969 and improved so quickly in downhill that he was appointed to the A Team and sent to Europe to race.

Inside his helmet Rudd heard nothing. There is not much noise to a downhill, just a whistling *swisssh* as the wind sucks past the racer. He glimpsed snow blurring around him, yellowed by his goggles. He pressed his weight evenly onto the two skis, to move faster. Because there were no trees with which to judge speed and distance, Rudd concentrated on the first difficult obstacle in this section, a bump that he had to prejump—to lift up his weight just before the bump so that he would land quickly and not be thrown in the air and lose speed. Immediately afterwards there was another bump, a bigger one, which he also had to prejump. Below it lay a long flat that dipped into a chute; then the course curved past the mid-station of the gondola lift that he had ridden up that morning.

Shadows hid part of the trail, making vision difficult, and Rudd smoked onto the bump quicker than he expected. He jumped, pitching his body up and forward like a ski jumper; then he lowered it into a crouch and pressed his hands forward, so his body would follow and the weight would force the ski tips down. The wind would hit the top of the skis, pressing them even more quickly onto the snow. Then Rudd would repeat the process for the next bump.

But he did not land where he expected; his skis just kept going, skimming through the air toward the next bump. Rudd remained about six feet in the air over the snow, a rushing blur of motion aerodynamically balled up to reduce wind friction. Rudd subconsciously knew he was overshooting the bump and the automatic reflexes that a downhiller develops started to function. Again he stood up on his skis, making a windcheck of his body to slow him down. But he remained airborne, hit the top of the next bump, and, like a stone skipped across a trout pool, was scaled higher into the air, over the hill, straight over the flat, twenty-five feet above the ground. His speed still produced the whistling swish as he hurtled through the air. He was no longer a ski racer in control of the mountain, he was a projectile.

During the previous day of training, Rudd had estimated his speed on this section at about sixty miles per hour. Overnight, the course had frozen harder, and the morning sun had not softened the snow. Rudd had made his first prejump at about seventy-five miles an hour. It was one small mistake, uncorrectable, that was leading him into a very highspeed crash and burn.

A spasm of fear, a clammy, cold wetness slammed into his stomach, then disappeared as Rudd tried to make a landing onto the flat. He kept his body stretched out vertically to break the wind, then prepared to absorb the shock of landing on the flat by folding his body, like an accordion. As his skis made contact with the snow, he used his body as a spring, folding his knees, then his back. But the force of gravity plus mass at seventy-five miles per hour was too much on the flat and his knees were forced into his chest, and his whole body was compacted, thrown forward. His face hit one of the ski tips and his jaw shattered in three places. Everything went black, and, like a dead rabbit worried by a hound dog, Rudd was shaken violently by the mountain.

As Rudd's jaw cracked and his face was mashed into the snow, his body hyperextended in a flip. His skis arched above him, then slammed into the snow tails first. One buried itself and Rudd was whiplashed into the snow back first. Two vertebrae cracked. The ski cracked too, the sound of dry pine popping in a picnic fire. Rudd flipped again, then slithered loosely down the smooth course until the speed was dead and he lay still, a dark, collapsed lump on the sun-bright snow. He had gone over two hundred feet in the air, one hundred feet on the ground.

In the time it takes to smile.

Many team coaches were huddled at these bumps, timing their racers and checking their prejumps. Willy Schaeffler was there, a Longines stopwatch in his hand, a Motorola radio slung across his shoulder. "God! He must be dead!" exclaimed Willy, and over the radio he called the team doctor, Rod Kirk, who was at the girls' slalom race. The young Canadian, Betsy Clifford, dressed in a red jump suit, was about to win her first World Cup race of the winter.

Stefano Anzi, the Italians' best downhiller, had also fallen at the same spot, but not seriously. He dragged Rudd to the side of the course so he would not be hit by the next racer. Stefano leaned over as Rudd regained consciousness and focused his eyes on the bright red-suited man with a pockmarked face. "Okay? You okay?" "Yeah," mumbled Rudd, and he got to his feet. Other racers had hurried onto the course and brought over his helmet, poles, gloves and skis, all of which had been ripped from him during the crash. The next racer, Marcello Varallo, swished past, a blur of

Betsy Clifford winning the women's slalom.

red—another shiny, red-suited Italian. The word had gone to the top—the course was fast, slow down.

Willy was on the radio with the doctor. "He's walking, I guess he's okay . . . No, he's walking in circles. Maybe he has a concussion. We meet you at the hotel." A Swiss doctor who knew the dangers of downhill training, and of this particular spot, examined Rudd, who felt he was all right. The doctor walked him several hundred yards to the mid-station gondola. Rudd rode it to the bottom and hitchhiked to his hotel, a five-minute walk from the mountain.

Betsy Clifford had won the girls' slalom and was surrounded at the bottom of the course by reporters and photographers. A grey silk scarf stuck out of her jump suit as she leaned over her poles. One hand moved nervously up and down the pole shaft but her face, smiling, happy, seemed to sparkle in the sunlight. Her eyes, grey and bright, darted from the reporters to the mountains, then back.

"Well, I almost blew it on the third gate of the first run . . . Yeah, I like to race, I see countries, learn languages . . . I hope to win the World Cup. Next year I think I can win three gold medals in the Olympics. Everybody does. Lot of pressure though, even if I win two . . ."

"Oh, she had an unbelievable second run," commented her coach, Peter Franzen. "She has plenty to go, she's only seventeen."

On her second run through the slalom course Betsy was unbelievably aggressive, fighting the gates, her mouth held in a sharp grimace, a pigtail streaming behind her. There is no doubt of her talent. She also plays the guitar, makes up lyrics, says and does what she likes. Some say she is a wild one. Her eyes never slow down, as nervous as a hummingbird, darting about. A few months before this race her younger brother was killed in a dune buggy accident.

As the press jotted down her comments, Rudd lay on his bed. His back and jaw were beginning to hurt, and the doctor wanted an X ray. The only machine big enough to photograph Rudd's back was in Bourg-St.-Maurice, twenty-eight kilometers away. Rod Kirk drove Rudd down the winding road, past Lac de Tignes and into the valley. The doctor from Aspen, Colorado, who donated his time and paid his own way to Europe to be with the team, had his diagnosis confirmed—broken jaw and two compressed vertebrae. Six weeks of recuperation and you're lucky it's not serious.

They wheeled Rudd onto the third floor of the hospital at Bourg-St.-Maurice, past a tray full of crusty bread, into a bare room with a sink, a white tiled table and two single beds with metal tubing hanging over the end, ready to support a traction break. The room looked like the morgue.

Rudd was on his back, an ace bandage holding his jaw in place. The only sign of injury was his swollen lips. The jaw did not hurt as much as his back. The nurse doped him for pain. He lay there, flat on his back, sometimes reading Vonnegut's *Slaughterhouse Five*, until his arms ached from holding the book over his head. His teammates visited, bringing oranges and jokes and smiles. They did not stay long. A hospital is a creepy place for a ski racer.

During the rest of the winter this room would be occupied with injured skiers, the refuse from Val d'Isère and other nearby ski areas—Tignes, La Plagne, Les Arcs—tourist skiers with wrenched knees, broken legs and ankles, the result of unused muscles fighting with unfamiliar skis. If they had taken a spill as Rudd did, on the OK piste at seventy-five miles per hour, they could be crippled, or dead.

Rudd was not missed at Val d'Isère, except by the Americans, because who ever heard of Rudd Pyles? And if an American is hurt and misses the season, well . . . a shrug of the shoulders . . . "It's too bad, but . . . they're just a bunch of amateurs." Besides, there were cocktail parties to go to. One for the press was given by Martell and Black and White, two of France's better selling cognacs and Scotches. Tiny, hot hors d'oeuvres were served by long-skirted, smiling hostesses.

The press in Europe is privileged and welcomed. Hotel rooms at various races are discounted for them, and if some do not get a room with a bath, they complain. The press invariably congregate at the finish line, as they had that morning at the girls' slalom, marking down times, listening for and promoting rumors. The winning racers are asked the same questions, race after race—"Did you have trouble on the course? . . . Was it fast? . . . Did you think you would have a chance to beat . . . ?" When the French skiers lose, the French press will invariably publish a statement saying why the French cannot win all the time. And the Austrians write about why the Austrians are not winning and talk about firing the coach, but they prefer to criticize the French, who usually do win. "And to what," minced Austria's leading ski journalist to French star Patrick Russel, after he took a spill in a slalom, "do you attribute your defeat?" There are the newspaper journalists, a middle-aged bourgeois group, and the TV people, who generally work hard, and the photographers, who spend much of their time hustling their pictures to the ski equipment people for advertisements. The press make heroes of winners and ignore losers. They could care less about an unknown American who cracked his back in training just as Betsy Clifford won her first race of the season.

Jean-Claude Killy doing his job for Head skis.

There was also a glamorous cocktail party hosted by the Evian people. It was the big event of the Val d'Isère races. Officials and politicians and coaches and beautiful women with beautiful clothes and ski equipment directors, presidents, vice-presidents, and even Jean-Claude Killy, mingled and drank Scotch and gin-and-orange juice and bit into the flaky hors d'oeuvres and made dates for dinner, a discothèque and hopefully a common bed. It was as glamorous as the movies. But there were no racers at the party; none had been invited. Later, at Jean-Pierre's, a small pub that is quiet and serves three-franc beer, Killy shared drinks with three girls, one of them an old-time aficionado of the race circuit. Killy worked hard during the day, promoting Head skis. Ex-racers who win big are invited to all the cocktail parties.

While the parties were flashing, the lights were extinguished in the hospital room where Rudd lay still, staring into the darkness. Before sleep came, Rudd thought about his crash and injury and the circumstances that led to it, and about ski racing, and a lost season.

Sunday, the day Rudd Pyles flew from Geneva to a hospital in Denver, was also bright and warm. The early temperature was − 8 degrees Centigrade, but as the sun rose it became sweater weather. There was none of that frightful, wind-seared cold that Bob Cochran was used to in Vermont during December and January. Bob Cochran was conditioned for cold. He never wore longjohns under his racing suit. He, like Rudd, wanted to win. He thought he had a chance, even though he was one of ninety-seven racers.

The course was fast, and throngs of spectators were standing near the difficult sections, waiting for a Sunday thrill. The first racer left the starting gate at eleven o'clock. Precisely. The Longines timing equipment rarely makes mistakes. The wand that starts the clock, after it is pushed forward by the knee of the racer, actuates an intricate integrated system

3. The Downhill

that prints out the seconds to the hundredth, simultaneously registers the same time on a billboard-size scoreboard at the finish and also on luminous digital indicators for transmission by the television camera. The racer's final time is frozen by a high-frequency modulated light beam that is broken when he crosses the finish line.

A spectator, keeping tabs with the announcer or the lit-up scoreboard, can mark the time of any racer at any interval during the race. Some racers are fast on top, some make it up at the bottom of the course, and it is exciting to witness a racer gaining, then surpassing the best previous time. Longines is proud of their system.

Most of the error is at the starting gate, and it is not the fault of the timers, it is with the racers; it is how they mobilize their body before the knee pushes forward the timing wand. For the start a racer relies mostly on mo-

Upper part of the Val d'Isère downhill with a solitary racer, the speck in the center of the shaft of sunlight, lower center.

bilizing the upper body with his arm and shoulder muscles so that it is in motion before the timing wand is opened by the knee. Using the poles as leverage, the body is lifted over the poles and the upper torso is bent forward, pushed into motion while the skis remain stationary. At the last moment, the skis are pulled in motion, following the fast-moving body, and the right knee kicks open the wand. By that time the racer is skating out of the gate. A good, fast mobilized start can win for a racer a couple of hundredths of a second and give him a psychological boost for attacking the course. Killy was the first to analyze the importance of the start. A second before his start, he jumped into the air, arching his body over the timing wand. Then he planted his ski poles into the snow and catapulted himself out of the starting gate, opening the timing wand with his ankles at the last instant. It was explosive, but the officials did not like this catapult start and now all racers must have their poles planted in the snow during the countdown.

As in training, the racers moved out at one-minute intervals. Each racer is rated, or seeded, against all other competitors in slalom, giant slalom, and downhill. This rating determines the racer's starting position. The racer with the lowest seed—the lowest number of points (called F.I.S. points, after the Fédération Internationale de Ski, the organization that computes them), starts first. A rating is compiled from the best two finishes in downhill, slalom and giant slalom events, and takes into account the competition. If the race has no low-handicap competitors, it is handicapped with a certain number of points. Each racer is trying to lower his points so that he will eventually be rated in the first seed of fifteen competitors. The lowest seeded, or best racers, not only start first but have a better course to race on.

Before a race, the starting position in each seed of fifteen racers is picked by lot during a coaches' meeting. In slalom and giant slalom there are two runs, with the winner determined by the lowest combined time. To even each racer's chances in each seed, running order is reversed for the second run. A skier who races first during the first run will race number fifteen in the second run.

Bob Cochran knew the starting procedure well; he had worked on it with his father, Mickey. A mechanical engineer by profession, a ski coach by inclination, Mickey Cochran developed procedures for the start and a table that describes the efficiency of different types of body position during a prejump. Bob and the rest of the top-seeded waited at the top of the course, all of them serious, a bit glum looking—the first wave on D-Day. The trainers loosened their muscles with rubdowns, technicians checked their bindings, and the racers worked on their own psyches. Usually one of the first fifteen will win the race, because they are the best racers and because the course is not yet rutted in the turns. Ruts force skis to chatter and make racers slide a bit, losing time.

Of the top fifteen, five were favorites: Bernard Orcel and Henri Duvillard of France, Karl Schranz and Karl Cordin of Austria, and the happy kangaroo, Malcolm Milne of Australia. Nobody considered Bob Cochran, running number eight.

Orcel, in a race suit the bright yellow color of his hair, slithered out of the start and tucked into the aerodynamic egg position to carry him over the flats. He is a handsome man with a stern yet sensitive face that turns on the girls. He also knows himself well and has trained his mind and body for "the love of speed, to go faster and faster" and for that intangible skill of being able to judge the maximum speed in relation to turns and bumps.

It is the same point that Karl Schranz picked out as an important skill of the downhiller, and it was one point Rudd Pyles was figuring out in his hospital bed.

Orcel, like the rest of the favored downhillers, is a *glisseur*—he rides his skis lightly. Except for Malcolm Milne, they all grew up in mountain villages. "When one wants to find a champion, look where the life is hard," said Jean Vuarnet, director of the Italian ski team and gold medal winner in downhill at Squaw Valley in 1960. "You find them in the mountains, in valleys, where ski racing is a step up the ladder. If you look to the city or the university, the students you will find lack the patience to become champions. They are too well equipped and do not have the temperament."

It takes eight to ten years and about $45,000 to produce a champion ski racer, assuming the racer has the potential. The Europeans who have it are usually out of school at the age of fifteen or sixteen and are apprenticed on the race circuit. Orcel, from the ski village of Alpe d'Huez, spent nine years training for downhill, and he was ranked seventh in the world during the '70–'71 season. A few years ago his body and mind became so nervous before a race as to hamper his performance. So he practiced yoga to make his legs and chest more supple and relax his mind. Still nervous before the start of a race, Orcel practiced breathing exercises to calm himself. He became so relaxed that in one race he was ten seconds out of first place, though he thought he raced well. The coach banned yoga. Now Orcel does yoga for ten minutes each morning, using the exercises to stretch his muscles, like a cat. Sometimes, after races, French team members go to their room and do breathing exercises accompanied by music. Every couple of years, Madame Ruchbaul, a yoga specialist, visits the team. But the French trainer in charge of conditioning, René Meallet, remains skeptical.

Orcel was very familiar with the OK downhill, and as a *glisseur* and technician he skied a perfect race until he came to what is known as "Emile's bump." He misjudged his speed, went high in the air, lost his balance, then regained it, and landed outside of the course, 120 feet below the bump. He controlled his skis, managed to get back on them, missing the trees, and continued the race. He finished second. He would have won, except for that one mistake.

Henri Duvillard—Dudu, as he is called—was on the course. The most perfect of the international skiers, talented in downhill and giant slalom, and improving quickly in slalom, he was a favorite to win the World Cup. A small man with bright eyes and a sharp chin, he makes up for his lack of weight with aggressiveness and technical ability. He likes to dominate the ground he is running on, to feel the snow as much as possible, savoring the speed. A Mégèvian from a family of ski racers, he has been racing since he was eight. His father is a ski instructor and the family farm is not far from Mégève's famous Mont d'Arbois hotel, where royalty and the haute bourgeoisie spend idle hours in their private, secured world. Duvillard was in the best physical condition of any member on the French team. He had won this race in 1968 and wanted to win again. But in a technical turn, a compression where the racer banks the turn under considerable G force, he missed his line and, for one horrible fraction of a second, lost his balance. His hand hit a control gate with a solid whack. He finished fifth and felt he was not attacking. His hand was broken.

The ski technicians, those who are responsible for maintaining skis, bindings and poles, swarmed all over Karl Schranz just before he raced. His racing number was firmly taped to his racing suit so it would not flutter and act as an air brake. The technicians checked his skis and made sure he was fitted securely into the bindings and that they were set correctly. Ski racers do not wear leather thongs or any other safety straps to hold their skis to their feet should they fall and their bindings release. They believe that if they fall at high speed, and the ski remains tied to their foot, the ski's sharp edges can give them nasty cuts. So they leave the ski free from their foot, and in many cases, the ski, after a racer falls, heads downhill by itself and becomes a lethal projectile that can injure a spectator.

The coach took a small bar of ski wax and waxed the edges of Schranz's skis and the boots. This would make the skis slide better when they were sharply edged into a turn. At thirty-two Schranz was the oldest ski racer, and the most successful—two World Cups, a room full of other trophies, a hotel and property in St. Anton, a 4.2 liter Jaguar. His photograph appears on endorsements for skis, boots, poles, cars, insurance. Some of his team members do not like him and wish he would retire. "I'll retire when they are able to beat me," he has said.

According to his coach, Hoppi, Professor Franz Hopplicher, "Karli has ten percent talent for skiing. The rest is work." In 1969 Karli was still learning. At the Mégève downhill he managed to lower his egg position

Bob Cochran running the Val d'Isère downhill.

two inches and worked hard on sliding his skis. In 1970 he was ranked second in the world downhill. Now, dressed in black, Schranz skied fluidly; there seemed to be no faults. He placed third, three-quarters of a second out of first place, and calmly signed a half dozen autographs before he left for lunch. He was expected to win his third World Cup.

Five minutes before his start Bob Cochran was throwing his arms about, rolling his neck, trying to relax his body while infusing his mind with aggressiveness. Two minutes before the start Hanspeter rubbed his back and legs to keep him loose and warm; if you start cold, you have had it. Bob, a tall nineteen-year-old with an easy smile, had done his homework. He had side-slipped the course, picked the line he intended to race, run the trail to learn the speed and how far the bumps would throw him. Forty-five seconds before his countdown he was in the starting gate, positioning his poles, planting them firmly. He had a good start and his 218-centimeter skis, rigged with strips of plastic on the top, called dampeners and meant to cut down vibration, rode quietly. Bob felt confident.

Touch is very important on the course, a feeling Cochran compares to having a magnet hold your skis to the snow, and as his speed increased Bob experienced the sensation of floating, a state of happiness, of riding in a vacuum, hypnotized to the course. Yet if he missed his line, he would not attempt to recapture the lost split seconds. Bob does not take chances, and he knows his faults—long turns, where he is apt to ride his inside ski too heavily, slide, and lose time. That was just what he did, and he finished ninth. His face, reddened by the wind, except for where his goggles protected it, tightened when he saw his time on the scoreboard; then he looked up the mountain. "I didn't pack enough into it, I could have been a lot wilder. I took the compression too early." "How do you think you would have done if you were on?" "If I were on? I would have won it. My training hasn't progressed too well. I'll be on in January."

Because of school, Bob had had only two weeks of practice before the season, compared to the five months of training the Europeans had undergone.

Malcolm Milne cut the photocell at the finish, sprayed up powder and ripped off his helmet. He had finished with only one ski pole.

"Did you see me? Did you see me? Why . . . why . . . I could have bloody well killed myself!" and he scrunched his eyes into an awful look of fear and gazed up the mountain. "I could have killed myself!" His face was beet red from the wind, his hair a mop of brown locks shooting in every direction. Malcolm is not messy, but at times he is a little distraught. He had just about killed himself, and he was very happy to be at the finish line saying, "I could have bloody well killed myself."

A few minutes earlier he was two miles up the mountain, in the starting gate, chewing gum. He had won last year. He expected to win this year.

"Phott!" and the big wad of gum, propelled from Malcolm's pursed lips, sailed in a nice parabola through the air and landed five feet from the starting gate, outside the track. Malcolm scrunched down over his ski poles, his heavy eyebrows slanting all over his forehead, his brown eyes practically spitting sparks as his large lips curved into a threatening grimace. He got the signal from the bearded timer. *"Aarrrrgh,"* he yelled fiercely, and charged out of the starting gate, an Aborigine on the attack. Malcolm is a tiger. He is also a kangaroo. He invented the kangaroo squat. Not on purpose. He was ranked as the fourth best downhiller in the world. He is Australian. *Australian,* not Austrian. He, like the American racers, is an "outsider" who is not supposed to win races on the European circuit.

The start for Malcolm was typical. He had just gone through a few stretching exercises to relax his body, then he programmed his mind to attack. Fear and speed turn him on.

"Fear? A downhiller with fear? If I had fear, I wouldn't race," said Karl Schranz. "I only have fear of doing badly," stated Orcel. "Fear? Never," said Duvillard. "I never considered it," asserted Rudd Pyles. "Oh, just a touch, but it goes quickly," said Bob Cochran.

"Racers say they have no fear?!" replied Malcolm in wonder. "Why, they're all bloody liars! I'm frightened to go down and I'm sure they are too." The year before, a reporter had asked Malcolm, after he won the Coupe Henri, whether he felt fear. "Of course!" he retorted, "from top to bottom!" A five-year veteran at twenty-two, Malcolm has developed into a technician and a *glisseur*. More than any racer on the circuit, he has the will and the determination to win. He has what Willy Schaeffler calls the "killer instinct."

Malcolm and his older brother Ross were brought up in Myrpleford, not far from Melbourne, on a tobacco, grain and cattle farm. The country is slightly rolling, somewhat similar to the hills outside San Francisco. Two hours from the farm are the mountains, and skiing. Malcolm took up skiing when he was nine, following his older brother Ross to the mountains on weekend jaunts from the private school they attended. In 1964, Ross left for Austria to participate in the Winter Olympics at Innsbruck.

A few days before the Olympic downhill Les and Dorothy Milne packed their clothes and with Malcolm, then sixteen, drove to Melbourne. They had reservations the next morning for a flight to Munich. They were going to cheer the Australian team, and particularly their son Ross.

The three checked into the Southern Cross Hotel and went out for a farewell dinner. They returned early to the hotel, for it is a long flight from Melbourne to Munich. The desk clerk handed Malcolm's father a cablegram. It stated simply that their son Ross had died that day of injuries received from a fall during the downhill training. There was nothing to do. They repacked and drove back to the farm and quietly made arrangements for the funeral.

The details they heard were sketchy. Ross was running the Patscherkofel downhill in training and some racers, or spectators, were on the course.

Malcolm Milne of Australia.

He made a quick check to slow down, caught an edge in the snow and his momentum thrust him into the air and over the bank of the trail. His face smashed into a tree. He died two hours later.

Over the next few weeks, Malcolm read about the accident in newspapers. The Australians and New Zealanders are not good enough skiers, commented one report. They should not be allowed to race on the A circuit in Europe. Malcolm was furious at what he considered slander to his dead brother. He quietly determined that he was going to be a downhill racer, that he was going to "show them all" and carry on where his brother left off. He promised himself that in five years he would win a World Championship and a major European race.

Malcolm started to race in Australia, and he became a good junior. His parents were not happy, but Malcolm is stubborn. Several of the French team members visited the Milne farm. Jean-Claude Killy, Léo Lacroix, and Marielle Goitschel were racing in Australia and they had come to pay a courtesy and sympathy visit. But it was a little more than that. They had

Milne in the starting gate.

heard of the young Milne and they invited him to train with the French ski team. The invitation was official with a letter from the French coach, Honoré Bonnet, and with the reluctant blessings of his parents Malcolm flew to the French Alps to live, train and race with the French racers.

He quickly found out that, compared to the French racers, his skiing was atrocious. But, he thought, if they can do it, I can. As he developed into a racer, Malcolm yearned to run downhill, which was specifically forbidden to him by his parents. He finally inveigled Bonnet to write his parents for permission to enter him in a very small, easy downhill. Permission was granted, again reluctantly, and Malcolm was on his way. For the next four years Malcolm worked on his seeding in downhill. He started with a racing number between 90 and 100 and, year by year, lowered it, until he was grouped in the first seed in 1969–70.

"God, it's frightening, the way youngsters take chances on the course. They don't know what they're doing. But if you get through the first few years of downhill, you can make it," Malcolm recalled. And this was what he did. He attacked every course and crashed often, because he was going too fast for his ability. It is in these years that accidents happen and force skiers to retire from racing. Malcolm made it. In 1969 he won the Coupe Henri at Val d'Isère. It gave him a lift, the best feeling he ever had, a floating high over his first major victory. He went on to win a third place bronze medal in the World Championship downhill (and made something of a non-prophet out of Schranz. "Pack your bags and go home," Schranz was reported to have said to Milne. "You'll never make a downhiller."). Malcolm had fulfilled the promise he had made to himself when he was sixteen. Sounds corny. But these Australians . . .

At the halfway point Malcolm was running hot; he had the fastest time. Then he hit Emile's bump and made the same mistake as Orcel—he misjudged his speed—and the bump threw him up in the air, about twelve feet, and like a stone propelled from a slingshot he sped toward the woods. Directly in front were two huge pine trees and a red-suited girl scurrying for cover. The wind forced one of Malcolm's skis up so the tip was pointing vertically. His weight went back and still he soared toward the trees. Then, with a tremendous effort, he forced his ski down just before he landed, outside the course, and slid down the track, sitting with his buttocks on the tails of his skis. He has done it so often, it has become known as the kangaroo squat. For sixty yards he skied as if he were riding a sled, holding his equilibrium with his hands on the snow. He forced himself up, lost a ski pole, and finished the course, still racing, though a bit awkwardly, thanks to the missing pole. No hit trees, no hit girl, in fact no crash.

"Did you see me up there, I could have bloody well killed myself!" and he looked with wonder and amazement at the mountains and the people he could still see and feel.

In some ways, Malcolm is very much like the Americans. He is relaxed and friendly; he does not have much spending money. He has been fortunate to have been trained by the French team, yet it was not the French who instilled in him that competitive edge that has made him into a winner. Few American ski racers have displayed that quality—the ability to surpass their physical or technical limitations through guts and will. The only American who could be compared to Malcolm was Buddy Werner, who raced the European circuit by himself in the late fifties and early sixties and shocked the Europeans by winning with no coach, little train-

Eric Poulsen placing seventh in the giant slalom.

ing, money, or technical backup. He, like Malcolm, was a beloved under-dog, but Buddy had something else too. He had the reputation of the *Crazy American.* To the European in the late fifties, all Americans were slightly crazy and could do anything they wanted. They were winners. World War II had not been forgotten. When the Americans started to field ski teams in the sixties, the results were bland, and the élan of the lone, crazy Ameri-can was gone.

The rest of the Americans ran. Mike Lafferty in thirteenth. Good. Rog-ers Little, twenty-seventh. Hank Kashiwa, thirty-fourth, Spider Sabich, the old pro, skied almost straight up, his poles dragging behind, just as the high-school kids raced back in the late forties. He was either very chicken, or he did not care—thirty-seventh. He prefers slalom anyway, and so does Steve Lathrop, fifty-fourth. Rookie Craig Shanholtzer placed fifty-ninth and Eric Poulsen, who did so well in giant slalom the day before (eighth) finished seventy-ninth, six places out of last.

Karl Cordin, the young Austrian, tall, blond-headed, bright blue eyes, a womanizer and raconteur about the details of him and her the other night,

Karen Budge and Marilyn Cochran with Willy Schaeffler.

won the race. He skied smoothly and did not look fast. His coach said if he could lower his aerodynamic position by three inches, he would be the best downhiller in the world. He already is.

The American girls did not do well in downhill either. The highest finish was Marilyn Cochran, sixteenth, and the rest finished from thirty-second to sixty-fifth, next to last—that was Penny Northrup, who skied with an injured leg. The women's coach, Hank Tauber, was riding her pretty hard. Hank is tough with the girls. Barbara Ann Cochran had already blown up at him in an outbreak of temper. But it was the beginning of the season, the Americans were not well trained, and Hank and Willy Schaeffler were getting heat from nearly all the team members. Both of them believed in discipline, and who ever heard of a young American, especially an independent ski racer, who likes discipline, regimentation, schedules, criticism and all that jazz? And racing, with all that discipline just for fun, with no money? Is that the way you do it to win?

The race was over. Rudd Pyles was on his way to Denver, to have his jaw and back put back together. The various teams and racer chasers

The women's downhill at Val d'Isère.

packed their skis, equipment, and caravaned out of town, and the day after the racers left the ski tourists flocked in, packed into buses and the family Renault. The ski school started operation, children's ski classes were booked full. The race was forgotten, and competition had moved from the downhill course to the lift line, where the ski tourists jockeyed for position.

The Americans split for the Christmas holidays and some practice racing, the girls to Nice, the men to Klosters, Switzerland, Hanspeter Rohr's
home town. The next World Cup race would be in the new year.

The snow that was supposed to fall before New Year's Eve never came. It was still sunny, warm and comfortable, and the skiers had to rely on the snow that had accumulated in early December. It was one of those skinny European winters. By February the grass would be turning green in the lowlands of Switzerland and farmers would be plowing their fields. Near Bern buds were sprouting on the trees. The men's and women's teams had started their separate circuits. The girls were off to races in Yugoslavia and Austria; the men started the New Year's season racing in Berchtesgaden— Hitler's old hideaway. The split between Willy's desire for teamwork and regimentation and some of the racers' desire for freedom came out in a confrontation between Willy and Spider Sabich. At Berchtesgaden, Spider had run the first slalom course and was disqualified. Willy was unhappy with Spider's performance.

4. A Race for Glisseurs

WILLY: You're not concentrating, an intelligent guy like you, you got a degree and some woodchopper that hasn't finished grade school can remember sixty-five gates and you can't? You can remember better than he and you keep getting disqualified. Why?

SPIDER: I'm standing in the slalom gates and I'm thinking of my classmates and some of them I know make twelve hundred dollars a month already and what am I doing here?

WILLY: That's the most honest explanation yet, and you better get out in a hurry, don't waste money. We have to look and find other kids.

Spider flew to the U.S. He was twenty-six and preferred to think for himself and not be bossed around by a coach. Back home he joined a new professional ski racing circuit that Bob Beattie, his old coach, had formed,

Spider Sabich after he turned professional.

and in his first race he won a check for $1,250. By the end of the season, he had earned $21,188.77 in prize money. He was happy, and no longer a loser.

"Spider's winning does not show how good Spider is," said Willy, "it shows how lousy the pros are."

Professional ski racing, as it is developing in the United States, is designed for television. There are two parallel courses, and two competitors race simultaneously in head-to-head competition. It is exciting to watch. The courses are short, so the race can be seen from one vantage point. Also, the courses are much easier than they are in international competition. The race course is similar to a slalom, but without as many gates and with maybe a bump or two built into the hill. There is no giant slalom or downhill racing. The racers compete in elimination heats until the finals. It is much like a tennis championship. Most of the European racers prefer to stay in the international circuit. There they can make more money, and the serious competition is on the World Cup circuit, not with the new professional league. So there was something to what Willy said.

When Spider flew home, two slalomists had just joined the team, Rick Chaffee, the team's unofficial captain, and Tyler Palmer, a young racer from New Hampshire, who surprised everyone in Berchtesgaden by placing fourth in the slalom that Spider messed up. They filled out the team that left Berchtesgaden for Madonna di Campiglio, Italy. It was a somewhat restless team after the Sabich-Schaeffler blowup, and rumors were floating that Hank Kashiwa and Mike Lafferty, a young downhiller from Eugene, Oregon, were going to quit and turn professional. In Madonna, the team's average finish was twenty-fourth in slalom and giant slalom, but the team stuck together, and, with quips about Willy's autocratic discipline, headed from Italy to Wengen, Switzerland, for the Lauberhorn championships. But no—Wengen did not have enough snow to hold a slalom and downhill, so they canceled and St.-Moritz picked up the race. The caravan of racers arrived there in the middle of January—a collection of cars and trucks, Peugeots, Volkswagens, BMWs, Mercedes, their ski racks loaded with stuffed, heavy ski bags, and the trucks and buses filled with more ski bags, and boot bags, and helmet bags. The team manager carried ski repair kits, huge fifty-pound sacks of waxes, bars of red, blue, silver, and yellow for all types of snow conditions, plus large chunks of paraffin, burners to melt the wax, files to scrape the edges, P-Tex sticks to fill in gouges on the plastic bottoms of the skis, tools for mounting bindings, cutting ski poles to size, repairing boots. Technicians from ski factories drove into town with backup sets of skis, plus all the equipment needed for maintaining the skis. Boot technicians arrived with extra boots and large supplies of buckles and machines to punch out sections of the boot if they were hurting the racer's foot. All these racers and their piles of equipment drove through the Engadine valley, up the winding road into St.-Moritz, a compact town nestled next to a lake and surrounded by the massive peaks of the Piz Nair, Corvatsch, Muragl, Diavolezza. St.-Moritz has luscious shops and beautiful hotels. The tourist skiers run a bit older than the Val d'Isère crowd and appear much more wealthy. Val d'Isère is a masculine town, slightly rough, virile, sexual. St.-Moritz is refined, feminine. The hills are graceful and not as steep as at Val d'Isère. After skiing you may go to a tea dance. A lot of old people ride on the snow-covered hillside roads in horse-drawn sleighs, with bells tingling.

The American team was staying in the Chantarella, a mammoth hotel with a view overlooking the town, lake and mountains. When the Americans arrived in their Peugeot bus and Willy's Mercedes they immediately filled the hotel's ski room with their equipment and checked into their rooms. Willy had assigned each racer a roommate, an arrangement which was not to everyone's liking. Shortly after arrival, as happened at every

51

Hanspeter Rohr, center, gives the team the next day's schedule in the ski room of the Hotel Chantarella.

hotel they stayed at, Hanspeter and Willy worked up a schedule and stuck it on the door to the ski room. It was generally the same: 7:00 A.M., up; 7:15, outside for a short workout; 7:30, breakfast; 8:30 on the hill for race or practice; 12:30, lunch; 2:00 training or race; 5:30, team meeting or repair skis; 7:30, dinner. Unofficial bed check was 11:00. It was a strict schedule, and anyone who was late received a sharp reprimand from Willy. This was also the first year that the American team had had to spend at least an hour a day preparing their own skis, filing edges, filling gouges on the bottom. Most European racers have technicians do this work. But Willy thought the Americans did not know how to prepare their skis, and a good ski racer should know his equipment. "Karl Schranz won't let anyone touch his skis," said Willy. "The Americans, for them to prepare their own skis is ridiculous," said a European racer. "They should be concentrating on winning races, not on their equipment. Does Jackie Stewart repair his own race car?"

The Chantarella is used to an older and more sedentary clientèle than the American Ski Team. The help is dressed impeccably in white during the day, black at night, and they serve good pastries. The bar is a long rectangular room filled with overstuffed chairs and quite often overstuffed ladies and gentlemen. The rugs are worn but of good fake Persian quality.

In a corner room on the third floor an elderly gentleman rested in a lounge chair on his small balcony, wrapped in a green blanket, his white, sunglassed face turned to the sun. He seemed to be dead. After each day of training, or racing, the skiers passed under the balcony and the blanketed man was always there, motionless. Maybe he was Goldfinger, or Doctor No.

Two floors higher, in a room strewn with helmets, racing suits, ski boots, suitcases, a portable radio-phonograph and books, Hank Kashiwa was lying on a masseur's table. His body is compact, symmetrically built, golden hued. He is, by test, the athlete with the quickest reflexes on the team, and he also attracts girls quicker than the other racers. Hank was twenty-five and in his third season in Europe. He was trying to put his head together on racing—he considered winning 50 percent a mental activity. A local masseur was loosening Hank's muscles. He finished with a brush job—rubbing Hank's body with a stiff-bristled brush, starting at the soles of his feet. Hank was so relaxed he could hardly move. His skin tingled. He had to get up for the downhill tomorrow.

In a nearby room Craig Shanholtzer, Shanny, was sitting on his bed staring at the wall, thinking. Sometimes he read—Hesse, Gandhi. He prefers to stay by himself. A few days earlier, at a B circuit race, which is run for the second-string skiers, he had placed second in the downhill. It was a boost, after his fifty-ninth at Val d'Isère. He also was waiting for tomorrow, getting up for the race.

So was the town of St.-Moritz. They had had a week to prepare for the races, to make a slalom and downhill course. They had called out the Army, the fire departments, the trail workers, the school children, and the ski school. Within four days they had manicured the downhill course, removing the bad bumps and packing the snow into a hard base. They had watered the slalom hill, packed it by machine, then foot, then with skis, and then they had salted the snow to make it harder. At the same time they found lodging for the racers, coaches, officials and press (with discounts of course), printed up race schedules and hotel lists so everyone knew where they were staying, organized cocktail parties, installed two telexes, set up sixty typewriters with tables in the gymnasium, and arranged a communication headquarters on the hill for the radio and TV people. Four days it took them. To pay for it they dunned every shop in town. The $32,000 the race cost was paid back in fifteen days, through television rights, spectator tickets, and shop business. In Maine, the scene of a World Cup race scheduled for February at Sugarloaf, planning started six months before the event.

While all this work was being done, and the non-stop downhill training was taking place, and the fire department was watering down the slalom hill, the Club Méditerranée's huge hotel, Lion d'Or, caught fire. The fire was first spotted by race officials on the downhill course. They notified the fire department on the slalom course (whose radios happened to be on the same frequency as the race officials'), who quickly packed their hoses and rushed down the mountain to the fire. Churchbells were ringing, sirens were screaming, ski racers were running downhill, while a huge mushroom of smoke climbed from the valley and burned off the haze.

"These Swiss," muttered Willy, looking at the smoke rising above the town. "They'll even burn the haze off to make a better race."

Four hours later, the detachment of firemen were back on the slalom course, watering it down, tramping down the snow. The fire was out of control; it was an old hotel, a firetrap, nobody was hurt, and it is more economical to let it burn to the ground. Besides, the race, it was very much more important.

The St.-Moritz downhill runs from the Piz Nair past the Alp Giop to the Oberalpina. It is 2,910 meters long and the time to run it is about fifty-five seconds less than the time for the OK trail at Val d'Isère. The Piz Nair runs through undulating terrain of smooth rounded mounds, each of them interlocking in a huge expanse of whiteness. These hills are sensual in their curves. There are no trees here; the rolling snow fields stretch in all distances, but they all dip into the valley at St.-Moritz.

The downhill course is also slightly feminine. It has a few fast spots, good rhythm and a number of flats. It is a race for a *glisseur,* one who knows how to ride his skis loosely, who can pick up speed on the flats.

The night before the race it snowed, not much, but the six inches were enough to soften the trail to the extent that the first seed of fifteen skiers had a slower track to race on—their skis packed or scraped off the loose snow, making the snow harder and faster for the rest of the racers. In addi-

55

(ON THE FOLLOWING PAGES) *Downhill training at St.-Moritz, while the Lion d'Or burns (smoke is visible in left center of the picture).*

tion, a slight haze obscured vision for the first fifteen or twenty skiers. The skiers farther down the seeding list actually had an advantage, something that happens about every five years, the veteran race watchers say.

The race was typically Swiss organized. Eight first-aid stations lined the course, serviced by three helicopters and one ambulance. The only serious injury in training occurred when Austrian Hans Kogler fractured his leg and was hauled off on the pontoon of a helicopter. Three loudspeakers along the course kept the 4,500 spectators informed of who was in front.

Hank Kashiwa, hidden under his helmet and behind his deep amber goggles, sucked air into his lungs, then deep into his diaphragm and held it there as he rolled his head back and forth. The air exploded out of him, and he stretched his body. It was a yoga exercise that brought blood to the brain. Hank was running number 56, and in a minute he would be on the course. Bob Cochran had gone down, and on one corner before a flat his skis slid, he lost his speed, and he finished sixteenth. Mike Lafferty, another downhiller, finished thirteenth, the same position he had at Val d'Isère. Swiss skiers were in first, second and third, and some were already calling the race the Swiss National Championships—eight Swiss were to finish in the first fifteen.

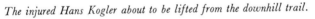

The injured Hans Kogler about to be lifted from the downhill trail.

Bob Cochran loosens up before the downhill.

The Swiss are very good *glisseurs;* they train with lots of free skiing, up and down their treeless mountains, covering all types of terrain, and they receive good support from their federation and their government. During the summer and fall the Swiss team spend every third week at a snow and physical training camp. In the two-week intervals they train at home with a conditioning program custom made by the coach for each team member. The Swiss are looking to the future. They recently hired a talent scout to find promising boys and girls, and in their plans is a national center where teen-agers can learn a trade and at the same time train for skiing. Ski racing is important for the Swiss. It attracts tourists, and a winning national ski team is a matter of national pride.

Hank, who is basically a slalomist in temperament and skill, used to consider himself too light (140 pounds) for downhill. Hanspeter talked him out of his pessimism and Hank was enjoying the challenge of downhill. In this race he pulled off his best finish—ninth. When you are starting from the fourth seed, this is like winning, and Hank wrapped himself in a big smile at the finish.

Hanspeter heard the good news over his radio at the starting gate, and he was all smiles as Craig Shanholtzer, running fifty-ninth, collapsed backwards into his arms, smiled lazily as he was lifted back to his feet. Shanny was loosening up and he can become very, very loose. He is a natural downhiller with an inbred talent that came to light when he trained with the team in November. He was not a member of the National Squad,

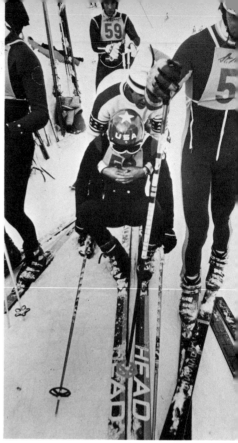

Karl Schranz is pampered before his run.

Hanspeter Rohr helps relax Hank Kashiwa. Shanny Shanholtzer (No. 59) awaits his turn.

but was on the Training Squad. Even so, Willy picked him to race in Europe. Shanny was nineteen, an inch under six feet and has brown eyes and brown hair. His eyes have a glint to them, and sometimes a faraway look, as if he sees something in the mountains that no one else sees. He is quiet, not really introverted, and at times he seems to be slightly cynical about the world. He could be a writer. One minute to go. Hanspeter was rubbing his thighs and calves. "Do I have fear?" Shanny replied. "I've asked myself that a million times and come up with a million answers."

"Shanny? I can't quite figure him out," said Hank. "Shanny? Unnnh, I dunno, he's a weird one," said another team member. "Shanny is an introvert," stated Willy. "He wants to be alone. He has everything in his favor; he has a good feel for the ski, you know, like a cat in the dark, putting his paw down. But he is opinionated. He dropped out of school and went to work for a farmer. That doesn't go in our game. Our game requires an unbelievable amount of self-control and discipline, and if you don't learn it, you will never be a racer."

Willy and Shanny are opposites. Willy believes in team regimentation, working together. Shanny believes in extreme personal freedom. He grew up that way. For the first eleven years of his life Shanny lived in Bosman, Montana, a college town of fifteen thousand. On weekends, the family, two sisters and a brother, his mother and father, would ski at a local area for fifty cents each. Business reasons moved the family to California.

Shanny, then in the eighth grade, did not like school in California any better than he had in Montana. "It was the same old garbage, partly discipline. We were a group of people in a huge school—moving one body of people from one room to the next and listening to so much bullshit and quoting someone else. You just took what they gave you. They taught you how to dress and wash." By the time Shanny was a senior in high school, he had picked up valuable racing experience on the Sugarbowl Ski Team and had become even more disgusted with school. They would not let him out for racing although he was keeping up his grades. Then, after a bout with mononucleosis, he did not receive help in makeup. "The administration was cowing the teachers, who wanted to help me. So I decided screw them and left."

His family, a close-knit one, agreed with his decision, and Shanny left for Jackson Hole, Wyoming, where his eldest married sister was living. In the fall quarter at Jackson Hole high school, he pulled off a four-point average. Then, with half a credit needed for graduation, he quit to go skiing. He has good board scores and can get into college if he wants to go. But his experience in high school has embittered him against further formal education.

In his first full winter of ski racing, Shanny was on the Wildcat, Colorado, ski team. Wildcat, a development near Aspen, was very promotion minded, but their business faltered and the team was disbanded. Shanny did not think he could afford ski racing and that summer worked in Jackson Hole for his brother-in-law, who exports Wyoming jade. "I had figured my ski racing had come to a screeching halt; then I got a call from the U.S.S.A. asking me what helmet size I wore. A screwy deal. I finally found out that I was on the Training Squad and was invited to train with the National Team at Aspen. So I'm here."

Shanny has few responsibilities—some car payments, rent. He is not

Shanny gets the 10-second countdown . . .

concerned with clothes; he dresses neatly in dungarees and blue work shirts. He is not a consumer and is not concerned with money, although he considers it unfair for the Europeans to be paid while the Americans are not allowed anything. "The American Ski Federation, are they screwed up! God are they naïve!" But Shanny rides with them, and he feels it is a good thing to cruise along while somebody else is picking up expenses. He likes it because he does not have what he calls the "get ahead and career attitude," a hangup that makes it especially tough for some of the older American racers.

Shanny's attitude is caustic of today's society. His politics are non-politics —"I wish they would go away, people lying and conniving and working for all the wrong reasons, working for someone's benefit which is usually their own." He wants to live a simple life and be more in touch with people.

Shanny believes the only good government is by the individual, and self-discipline is the only good discipline. "There is no way to justify discipline employed by one person or another." And that was where he, the team spirit, and Willy Schaeffler did not mix well.

. . . And is on the course.

"I can't stand to have people tell me to do things I'm going to do anyway, then making a schedule of it. I'm not going to do them in their order. It's like kindergarten—seven o'clock you are up, seven fifteen you are running, seven twenty-five you are at breakfast. Five minutes late and you get a smart comment. Trivia! All that should matter is how you are progressing as a racer, and as a human being.

"If they say I have to prepare my skis before dinner, I'll make it a point not to have my skis ready before dinner. If they say you can't go out and have a beer, why, I'll probably go out and have a beer. I don't like it when it gets to be a rebellion thing but sometimes it just gets that way."

Shanny believes Willy is a very sincere person, but he also believes skiers are individualists who do not function best in a regimented life.

Shanny had a good, strong start. His body was moving fast before he tripped the timing wand, and he skated onto the flat. Most racers pole and skate three times out of the start. Shanny poled for the first two, then skated by swinging his arms three times without using the poles, getting his speed from his legs, which are long. Then he tucked low into the flat, relaxed his knees and ankles, and in twenty seconds prejumped a sharp

knoll, extended his upper body, sucked in his legs and landed on the downside, pressing down with his feet so the spring in the skis would accelerate him forward. From the starting gate he appeared as a tiny gnat floating in air, then he disappeared from sight, over the knoll. In the distance smoke was still rising from the destroyed, smouldering hotel.

Below the knoll was another flat and Shanny, feeling the snow, looked at his ski tips. They were wobbling slightly, which is a good sign; he was not riding his edges, slowing his skis. In training, Shanny feels wind and cold, but during a race he remembers no sensation, not even of breathing except when he hits a bump and his wind is forced out in a loud *whoosh.*

Shanny hit a fall-away and took a schuss into a compression gully. This threw him back on his heels—too far—and he could not absorb the compression in his legs. But he held on and did not lose time as the course changed direction, then snaked to the left, a long and sharp turn which had to be skied hard or the skis would drift from their course. Halfway point. During training the day before Shanny had had the fastest time here.

Shanny knew, at the halfway point of the Piz Nair, that he could go faster, but he threw the thought out of his mind; he did not have the experience. He let his skis slide just a bit on the curve and held a good high line that sped him through the next turn and onto the flats. At this point he was slower than during training, and he began to make up for it here, staying loose, holding his turns on the outside ski and keeping the outside arm down, close to the snow, which kept his weight on the downhill ski and gave his body more angulation to hold the turn. On the flats he hit a roll, was up in the air, tucked, landed. Then he hit the fastest part of the course, and he felt his speed was close to seventy-five miles per hour. Chatter marks and ruts on the trail jiggled his body, and the sky, snow, and gates became a jagged blur of blue, white and red. His skis began to shake and he tried to absorb the pounding through his body; he felt as though he was being whipped about by a hopped-up vibration machine. He was over the roughness and his skis quieted down and the course came back into focus as he hit a small bump—a kicker—that he prejumped well. He hit a good position in the air, arms out front, together, his knees in his chest. The skis carried him through the air for seventy-five feet, but only four feet off the snow. He landed lightly and kept accelerating down the schuss into a swale with another kicker and a change of direction. It was hard to hit,

Racer in pre-jump 20 seconds after the start. St.-Moritz is barely visible in the haze.

but he was on target and moved onto the flats. Willy was there with his stopwatch, and he reported over the radio to Hanspeter, "He held his line beautifully." Shanny was having a very fast run; he was riding the snow closely, in touch with it.

"The satisfaction of running downhill and the satisfaction of making love to someone I really care about are probably pretty similar," Shanny said, trying to explain his emotion for downhill. "The mind and body are in super close contact, the mind is everywhere in your body and not just in your head. There is a complete awareness. Each part of you is making its own decisions, and it is at this point I don't know how much confidence I have to control my body with my mind. A lot of it is instinct. But to explain the physical sensations of downhill is really, you know, how do you explain sex to a virgin?"

Still riding a flat ski, Shanny hit another bump and flew off it longer than he had in practice. He realized the course was fast as he hit another bump, flying a hundred feet, but again he maintained a good position and landed lightly and there was little friction at impact. He lost little time. A rough side hill, a small change of direction, a dropoff, and Shanny was pressing the bumps, trying to accelerate. He rode over a washboard lightly so as not to be kicked by the roughness of the snow, another trick of the

Racer in the "egg" position at 65 m.p.h. His head and shoulders are a little too high.

glisseur. Some never learn it; they crash and scrunch their way down the mountain using force. They never make good downhillers, perhaps not good lovers either.

On the last hard turn of the race, ruts formed from the previous racers' skis forced Shanny's skis into small rolls that knocked him back on his heels. He lost his line and almost fell, but pushed his weight forward and caught his balance as he hit the flat that ended at the finish. He had made his first mistake, and he had blown the race.

A downhiller's concentration is so great that his mind, working like a programmed computer, unravels that ribbon of downhill into dozens of problems. The mental computer automatically tells the body what to do, how to react. The good downhiller becomes so efficient that he can change the programming during the race for certain conditions or obstacles—a change in the texture of snow, for instance.

Shanny, seven hundred yards from the finish of his fourth downhill of the season, was aware of the noise, although his mind refused to recognize it. He hit the finish line, smoked the snow into a fast stop, snapped loose the second and third buckles of his boots to release the pressure, loosened his helmet, and looked at the scoreboard for his time. He knew he had blown the race on that last turn, but he also knew he had run a good race.

Lange's Paul Carlson congratulates Shanny on his fifth place. Rogers Little (right) is also all smiles . . .

Then he heard the noise of about two thousand spectators cheering, and the racer-chaser who cared for his skis, Paul Carlson, jumped on him and wrenched him in a big bear hug, and Hank and the other team members were all over him. He had placed fifth and the crowd knew, because of the digital scoreboard, that he would have won the race if, on that last turn. . . . Shanny was out of first place by 60/100ths of a second. It was a real shocker for an American to do so well, for Hank Kashiwa to finish ninth and the rookie to finish fifth, both out of the fourth seed, but the Swiss like an underdog, and a few racers later they would go crazy in excitement and happiness when one of their countrymen, Manfred Jakober, running sixty-fourth, placed sixth. What a beautiful day for upsets.

"Shanny, I am proud of you," Willy's voice crackled out of the radio. Later, at the hotel's outdoor restaurant, Willy came up to Shanny, picked him up and gave him another bear hug and a big smile and a handshake. It was a happy moment for the U.S. team, and the rebellion and generation gap between racers and coach disappeared in the glow.

Shanny, warmed by the high St.-Moritz sun, just sat in the red slatted chair, leaning over, holding his head in his hands. He had a big happy, stupid smile on his face. So did Hank. Overhead, the green-blanketed sunbather was also taking the sun, motionless. He had not moved during the morning of the race.

. . . As is Hank Kashiwa.

Shanny savors the high point of his racing career.

Rick Chaffee and Tyler Palmer, the two skiers who joined the team in Berchtesgaden just before the Sabich-Schaeffler confrontation, are both slalom specialists. Rick Chaffee is a five-year veteran of the team. He has curly blond hair, pink skin, a shy smile, and wears gold frame glasses over his blue eyes. He is a consistent performer and can be counted on to place in the first ten in slalom, although he rarely has broken through the top three places. He does not like downhill and does not race in that event. At twenty-six he was the oldest on the team and was considered the team captain. After arriving in Berchtesgaden and listening to complaints from his team members about too much discipline and regimentation, he sat down to talk with Willy in the overstuffed chairs of the Chantarella Hotel. Rick told Willy that the team members were not happy, they had no time to themselves, they could not go out at night, the schedules were too stiff, they

5. The Victory

would like to pick their own roommates. Willy listened, then leaned forward in his chair, balled his fist, and banged it lightly on his knee as he talked.

"I told you all, in Aspen, this is no trip for fun. We are behind in conditioning and in training. And I lay down the rules. That's final."

Rick persisted, not quite as strongly, and Willy finally agreed to relax a little, if the team started to catch up to the Europeans.

Tyler Palmer is known as a bit of a wild one, sporadically good in slalom and pretty lousy in downhill and giant slalom. His reputation started with a bang in 1970 when, in a *Life* article called "The Flake and the Old Man," Tyler—the flake—was contrasted against veteran ski racer Billy Kidd. The article depicted Tyler as a casually dressed rookie who would make wisecracks at the wrong time, play practical jokes on the French rac-

ers, and polish off a bottle of wine after a race, while Billy Kidd was "scrubbing out his mind." The article was fair enough except that Billy Kidd went on to win a Gold and a Bronze medal at the World Championships and the victory seemed to infer that the wild, flaky, rookie would never make it. Actually, Tyler had a very good first year in Europe. In one slalom race he placed fifteenth after starting in the last seed—ninetieth.

"Hell," said one of his teammates from the previous season, "after that article came out, Tyler really started being a flake."

"Did you really polish off a bottle of wine after the race?"

"Hell, yes," snorted Tyler, "but the article didn't mention that the rest of them did too, except Billy." Kidd was onto something else.

Ruben Tyler Palmer III, out of Kearsarge, New Hampshire, a collection of a few houses stuck in the middle of the White Mountains: angular of build, quick of movement but awkward-looking, wiry, with russet colored hair, freckles, and a crazy teasing glint lighting his hazel eyes. Pointed chin and pointed nose. He could be a young Yankee farmer, working the cows on a rock-strewn hill; come every Saturday, he dusts down to the local square dance, picks out a dolly and gets a bit *likkered* up. Hell . . . yes! Just achin' for a hassle. They would call him Rube.

The U.S. Ski Association did not think much of Tyler. In their annual biographical sketch of the American team members, boys and girls, Tyler received the least amount of space for a writeup. "Expert and determined competitor who has a lot of talent in slalom," commented Willy Schaeffler. After the Berchtesgaden slalom, where Tyler placed fourth, a European coach summed up the Americans. "They are a surprising phenomenon," he said, "one has the impression that there are some good possibilities there . . . then there is nothing."

They shrugged off Tyler's finish. Another fluke. A rumor drifted through the team that Willy was interviewed about Tyler by a German radio announcer. "He's sort of a hippy," Willy supposedly said, "who won't do much." In the next slalom race, at Madonna di Campiglio, Italy, Tyler placed thirtieth. He was already forgotten.

Slalom is a young man's race. It is an effort of quickly released energy, a sprint. It is a nervous race, with quick precise movements and fast reflexes where the racer is working for 1/100th of a second as he turns around very closely set gates. While the downhiller is moving at sixty to seventy-five miles per hour for up to two and one half miles, making carefully edged

The veteran Rick Chaffee.

Tyler Palmer, typically clad, studies the slalom course.

turns and riding a flat ski, the slalomist is running about one third of a mile at about thirty miles per hour, carving abrupt short turns. The psychologists say that the best slalom racers are introverted, and not as aggressive as the calm, extroverted downhiller.

Unlike the procedure for downhill, slalom and giant slalom's winning time is based on a combination of two runs. At St.-Moritz, the first slalom course had 59 gates, the second 61—120 controlled turns. The slalomist must carve very precise, quick turns, and success depends upon how fast and efficient each turn is. A skier makes one small mistake, misses a gate, and he is disqualified.

On the Sunday morning of the St.-Moritz slalom, another clear, sunny day, the American skiers shouldered their skis and walked from the Chantarella, under the silent, immovable man on the third-floor balcony, up the curving, snow-covered road to the slalom course. The race was set for eleven thirty, but the racers were on the hill at nine thirty to walk up the course and study the line they would take through each gate.

Of all the racers, Tyler is by far the sloppiest; clothes just seem to flop on him, get torn and otherwise distressed. On this day he was wearing a pair of navy blue stretch pants with a light blue stripe on the side. The stripe was ripped in places—from banging into slalom poles—and the pants were rumpled around his boot top because he does not like the strap fitted under his heel. The pants originally belonged to Jim Heuga (Heuga and Billy Kidd are the only American men to have won Olympic medals in alpine skiing), who in the fall gave them to Tyler. The U.S.S.A. had outfitted Tyler with a pair of bell-bottom ski trousers, which he does not like to race in. Tyler's shirttail was sticking out from underneath his white, starred team sweater, which all members wore during races. His goggles hung around his neck and his racing bib—number 25—was tied in a tangle around his middle.

Each gate was numbered, from the top of the course to the finish. The racers started sidestepping up the hill, stopping to memorize the gates into a section, imprint it into their brain, then sidestepping farther up the hill. Tyler was friendly with the French racers, and two of their best slalomists, Jean-Noël Augert and Alain Penz, acted as Tyler's unofficial coaches. They pointed out little things—a tricky gate, and whether to cool it and how, and where Tyler slid too much in his turns. They like him, for he epitomizes the American—loose, wild, fast, eager, friendly.

The course was so hard that it was impossible to walk up it. The continual doses of water had packed the snow and smoothed the hill into a hard surface of granular snow. Without finely honed edges, a skier would slide to the bottom, as his skis would not bite and hold in the crust. There are five square inches of metal edges on the bottom of a ski and these edges are evened with a ten-inch file so they are flush with the bottom of the ski, and then squared off and sharpened, so they bite into the snow. Then, Carborundum is used to smooth the metal. Skiers, like bobsledders, know that a burr or knick on these thin strips of metal can slow them down. Knowledgeable ski technicians know that if a pair of skis has tips that oversteer, the edge can be tapered near the tip so it does not grab into the snow and react too quickly (many female racers use beveled edges that slow their speed). A racer who knows how a ski reacts to torque and flex readily realizes what is wrong with the ski and can correct it.

Tyler likes his edges very square. He uses Dynamic skis that have what is called a cracked edge. For the length of the ski, the edge is serrated every inch. These tiny cracks in the edge act as a shock absorber, allowing the ski to torque and twist without the stiffness and spring of a solid piece of metal rsisting the torque. Fiber glass skis have such resiliency and ability to carve a turn because the ski bends evenly from tip to tail and a solid metal edge limits the resiliency. Most racers now use skis made of fiber glass and metal, or fiber glass and wood, or a combination of the three. Newer fiber glass or plastic skis have no wood in them—compressed air fills the core of the ski, and the only metal is in the edge. Head and Rossignol were the first to introduce these skis, and some technicians claimed that the Swiss downhillers' successes were due more to the new ski than their skill. For slalom, these new skis can weigh as little as four and a half pounds each. The downhill skis are longer and, for the sake of speed, much heavier. Some of them are weighted with lead in the core and weigh twelve pounds a pair. During the season, Tyler Palmer uses a half dozen skis for the three events. His slalom skis are carefully selected for evenly balanced bottom and side camber, or spring, and for the flex of the ski. If there is too much pressure in the ski near the tip, the tail of the ski slides away; if there is too much pressure on the tail, or under the foot, the ski has a tendency to go straight down the hill and is hard to turn. Tyler rides evenly over his skis, so they are of normal flex and camber.

Tyler leaned on his poles and gazed down the part of the course he had studied. He skied down a few gates, looked down again, and started sidestepping back up the hill, past the spectators that were lining up along the edge of the course. It was warm, and some had brought their lunch. The parents and other relatives of the Swiss racers were there, urging on their kin.

Tyler's mother and father are both certified ski instructors who teach at Wildcat Ski Resort in New Hampshire. At first they did it for fun to have their children—two boys, two girls—ski free. But in 1970 Tyler's father was let go from his engineering marketing job with a Massachusetts firm—a victim of the economy. Ski instructing became their vocation. Nowadays, there is not much money in the Palmer household. Bob, Tyler's father, learned to ski at Tuckerman's Ravine at Mt. Washington when he was a student at Yale. He was a semi-pro baseball player, as was Mickey

Cochran. He is quick to speak his mind and Tyler, stubborn and sometimes obtuse, was always fighting with him. Tyler, who reflecting on this
period is apt to call himself "a badass and wild mother," pulled back as he
became more serious about racing. "I was the extroverted one, and Terry
[his younger brother] was more introverted. Now, we're a little closer in
temperament." Outside of skiing, Tyler grew up like most other American
boys. He started caddying in the third grade, when the golf bag was bigger
than he. He served a short apprenticeship as a soda jerk, worked on a construction crew, and on weekends did a bit of beaching and motorcycle riding. Tyler began to ski when he was in the third grade. For two years his
father sent him to Holderness, a private school in New Hampshire. To be
on the ski team, Tyler had to compete in cross country and jumping,
which he considered a waste of time. He did not particularly dig the
preppies, had a few fights, and in two years transferred to a public school,
where he could concentrate on slalom. He and Terry, now himself one of
the top racers in the United States, competed against each other, fighting
to win. At first, Terry was the better skier, then Tyler caught up when
Terry broke his leg. The two Palmers would compete against Steve Lathrop, another New Hampshire boy and top slalomist, who also was on the
national team and racing at St.-Moritz. Tyler worked his way up—he
took first in the New Hampshire slalom championships, then he was first
in the east. In 1967–68, a time when Tyler still considered New York City
as Out West, he went to Bosman, Montana, for the Junior National
Championships, and won the Combined. Tyler was twenty, and for most
of those years he had lived and breathed slalom racing.

It took over an hour for Tyler to study the course and imprint it on his
memory. By the time he reached the top, he knew each gate—the hair-
pins, two closed gates set vertically down the hill; elbows, one gate offset
against another; the flushes, four closed gates set close together, vertically
on the hill. Each gate is made up of two flagged slalom poles which are
planted in the snow about ten feet apart.

Not until the present season had Tyler ever studied a course. He had relied only on his reactions, a fact that would have shocked other slalom racers. But the previous summer, racing in Australia, he had begun to analyze the gates and managed to finish fourth in two races. Tyler learned
something else in Australia. He had a habit of bumping the gates with his

legs and shoulders when he ran a course, spewing slalom poles all over the hill. This did not disqualify him, as long as he kept both skis inside the poles, but the gate keepers had a busy time and Tyler, after a slalom race, was a sore mass of black and blue marks. In Australia he learned how much time he was losing by banging into the gates so hard, and that it was not necessary to end up a race bruised.

Tyler was racing in the second seed, and while waiting he skied beside the course, loosely, getting into the mood. Before him in the first seed were three super slalomists, two of them French. Last season Patrick Russel and Jean-Noël Augert had finished one-two in World Cup standings in slalom, followed by the young Italian prodigy, Gustavo Thoeni. Russel had missed winning the combined World Cup title last winter by three points, and he was the favorite to win this year. He had extraordinary balance and is recognized as the best athlete on the French team, as good in slalom as in giant slalom, and fair in downhill; he considers himself a very poor *glisseur*. An accountant and the most educated member of the French team, he is charged with nervousness. He can become quite depressed when he does not do well.

Patrick's method of racing has, in a way, revolutionized ski racing and ski technique. He skis with his body far back, and he pushes down with his weight to flex the heels of the skis on the snow so that they act as a spring, squirting him forward. Because of his agility, Russel can shift his weight quickly and change directions, sometimes when he is in the air. This style has now been refined into the French Ski Technique and is called *avalement*. Because of it, ski boots came to be designed with backs that ride halfway up the calf of the leg. These high backs distribute the pressure evenly over the leg. (When Tyler and his brother were in high school, they also devised highbacks, using flat sticks, to ease the pressure on the back of their legs.) For the joe-blow skier, it is now the thing to ski with one's weight way back—copy Russel. A few years ago it was a technical sin.

Russel's technique also calls for a different style of skis. Slalom skis formerly were stiff in the tips and in the tails. They were rugged. Now the tips are soft in flex and the tails are very stiff. Russel skis on Rossignols, a French ski of course, and they are custom-made for him. His skis have much more camber behind the heel, which gives him more spring—Tyler probably could not ski well on them.

Rossignol works hard producing racing skis. They have a special work-

Patrick Russel displays the technique that helped him place second to Jean-Noël Augert in the 1970 World Championships.

shop to manufacture competition skis for the twenty-five top racers in their ski stable. There are three different models for slalom, four for giant slalom and three for downhill. These skis are tested for efficiency during the summer and fall at Val d'Isère and Chile. Rossignol technicians use Omega timing systems to judge the speed of the skis under controlled conditions. With this data they determine weight, structure, profiles, camber, resistance to snow, and how to distribute the flexibility of the ski over its length.

By the fall, every French team member knows exactly what type of ski is best for him, and the skis are then manufactured. Each French racer on the national team has at least fifteen pairs of skis to use through the winter. The company believes that by supporting ski racing, they can make better skis for the public, and by advertising the racers who win on Rossignol, the public will like their skis even better. Head, K2, Fischer, Sideral and the other ski companies work on the same system. What is good for the racer is good for you. Technically, that is true.

Augert was on the course. He skis smoothly with his skis always on the snow. He knows when to put his weight back and squirt his skis. He has a timing mechanism in his head that tells him when to press and when to cool it. Today his mechanism was fouled up and he finished his first run poorly—seventh. Russel was down, flipping quickly and lightly through the gates; his form seemed to defy gravity. He was very fast—first. Thoeni zipped down, arms and body low, skiing fluidly and with grace. He does not look fast but he is. Third. A Swiss, Edmund Bruggmann, his country's best slalomist, pulled in second, and the spectators, 99 percent Swiss, cheered wildly. Chaffee and Kashiwa had good runs, eighth and twelfth.

Hanspeter was at the starting gate, rubbing Tyler's legs, speaking to him softly, giving advice. Tyler listens at times, but now he tuned him out. Teammate Eric Poulsen had just left the starting gate and had fallen. Tyler, who was next, jumped into the starting gate. He had not eaten breakfast, as is his custom on race days; he believes the food draws blood into his stomach, and he wants it in his brain. Tyler did not flash back the course through his memory; he went over a few technical points with himself—lean forward, make solid pole plants, keep your arms forward, stay on the downhill ski, go like hell! Go like hell! He had the countdown and was on the course.

In the fall, Tyler learned two important facts about his slalom skiing. Jim Heuga, the Olympic slalom medalist, noticed that he was not planting his ski pole at the beginning of his turns. He was coming up with the pole but not seating it in the snow and using it as a pivot to make the turn. Instead, he was swinging his ankles and arms. Tyler practiced pole planting and picked up time. Dick Dorworth, the National Team's assistant men's coach, told Tyler to stop being so precise, trying to make every turn just right. "Ski wild and loose," he said, "ski over your head a bit." Tyler could not believe it after he tried a few runs. He was faster. If he skied technically, he came to realize, he skied slowly. By skiing fast, he remained loose and relaxed. "Hell," he said, "I'm skiing my personality now. Hank and Rick, they're neat in their style, and so was Billy Kidd—very precise, very economical. Man, I ski the way I am."

Tyler looked a mess as he raced, hard quick movements with angular, exaggerated form. He lost a tenth of a second with a bad start, kicking the wand open too early, but now he was concentrating on going faster and faster, and the tough sections of the course were blurs.

Tyler skis straight to the gates and makes his turns closer to them than does any other racer. He tries to keep his skis on the snow, and unlike Russel he likes to have his weight right over the middle of his skis when he turns; he wants to feel the pressure on the tips; then after the turn he sits back and squirts his skis forward for the next gate. Tyler was skiing well, riding a flat ski, he was on his edges quickly, then off them and into the next turn. Each turn he made was carved, and his skis were not skidding on the hard snow. At the halfway mark he had one of the fastest times, and the announcer started the countdown as Tyler worked his way through a flush and poled through the finish. He was cheered loudly by several thousand spectators gathered at the finish—the unknown American racing twenty-fifth had finished in second place. Tyler looked at the scoreboard, searching for his time. He knew he had not made a mistake, except at the start. Then he realized that he was trailing the winner of the first heat, Patrick Russel, by one second. That was a large margin, and Tyler was not pleased.

Tyler Palmer on the first run of the St.-Moritz slalom . . .

There was a fifteen-minute break, then Tyler was walking up the second course, parallel to the first. Concentrating on the combination of gates, he blotted out completely from his consciousness his first run, and Russel's one-second lead. By the time he had sidestepped up the course, he even knew which slalom poles were warped. As Tyler waited to start his second run, he had been on the hill for four hours.

Russel was the first racer down the second course and on the last gate he caught a tip and was disqualified. Tyler was in first, and he had twenty minutes to think about it.

Most racers, those who are young and do not have many important races behind them, improve their seeding over the season, and Tyler was no exception. In the '69–'70 season he had moved from the sixth seed in slalom (running about ninetieth) to the fourth seed (thirty-sixth). During the summer he picked up F.I.S. points in races in Australia and he started the '70–'71 season ranked twenty-fourth in the world—second seed. Moving into the first seed is difficult but there is another psychological barrier even harder to crack, and that is finishing in the first three positions. It is a matter of concentration and skill, of being able to put two winning runs together. Many racers never do it. There is the pressure after a good first run—from teammates, the press, the crowd, and within the racer—to do well, to really bomb the second run, to win. Most racers become nervous and uptight, and buzzing in their heads is the thought of matching or surpassing the first run or the skier who has you beaten by a few tenths. When this happens, a racer is not skiing with his ability but with his emotion, and it does not work. The good racers, those who make it to the top, can take this pressure because they concentrate on the task before them—the running of one course, to ski it as well as possible, perhaps a little more than that. It is a matter of flushing the pressure from the mind and concentrating on your own abilities. It takes experience, and for a young American racing in Europe it is difficult. "Europe's not meat nor fish," said Tyler, "and you can't make it until the second year, then you go. You hear about Europe, those long downhills and those French and Italians winning, and you're psyched out. I fell all the time last year because I couldn't concentrate. You have the exceptions—Duvillard and Thoeni and Killy who are fortunate to have everything come all at once. Me, I'm no prodigy."

Usually, the second slalom race is finished after the first fifteen skiers have completed the course. They have the best times and there is little chance for a second-seeded skier to break through. At this race, on the Alp Giop, the racers and the press and crowds were waiting for Palmer to run. A second-seeded slalomist rarely is in first place after the first run, and hardly ever, ever wins. Almost everybody expected to see the unknown American tear down the hill and make a spectacular crash.

Palmer blocked the thought of winning out of his mind. "Forget it," he said to himself. "Have a good run. Ski like hell." There was no noise as Tyler started his second run, except for the announcer counting off his time. The course was still hard and the spectators near the gates could hear the scratching of Tyler's skis as he edged them in the ice, released the edges, then set them again, rasping into the snow, controlling his speed. At times it seemed as if he was leading with his chin, and his body angulated wildly in the turns. He dipped into a flat, out of sight, then the slalom poles, sticking over the top of the hill, started to wiggle as Palmer, like a fish in the weeds, slithered through them. He had not fallen, he was fast and the spectators were urging him on with quick cadenced shouts that matched Tyler's turns—*Op!-Op!-Op!* Tyler hit the last pitch of the course, knocked down three gates and poled himself wildly through the finish. The crowd could not believe it; he had not fallen.

Tyler had put together two perfect runs, the first time in his life, and he had beaten them all—Thoeni, Russel, Augert, Bruggmann—the best slalomists in the world. The crowd went wild—another upset—and Tyler was mobbed by his teammates. He was still out of breath but laughing along with Rick and Hank, who finished seventh and eighth after their second run. Another American team victory. Then the press moved in; they did not know anything about the American, "And your name is spelled how? . . . You live where? . . . How do you spell it? . . . How old are you? . . . And you learned to ski where? . . . What do you do for relaxation? . . . Did you think you would win? . . . What did you think of the course? . . . A friend yelled over, "Hey, Tyler, you going to call home?" "Naw!" he replied, "I don't have the bread."

A representative from the Bogner skiwear company saw Tyler standing in the middle of the press with his shredded ski pants. "A champion should not be dressed like that," he said to Willy. "We will make him two pairs." Tyler was led away to a German radio announcer who could not speak English, and Tyler responded with a number of *Ja's*. Patrick Russel con-

. . . And as he hustles to victory during the second run.

Rick Chaffee, left, and Hank Kashiwa are pleased with their results, and the team victory.

gratulated him. "That old fart," Tyler said later. "He cooled that last run. He went so slow he wouldn't have won even if he hadn't disqualified. He should have known better than that." Patrick, twenty-five years old, yearning to win the World Cup after his second-place finish the year before, was having trouble during his second runs; he was falling or missing gates. Jean-Noël Augert, with a big crazy smile, came over and shook the hand of his American friend. "Tyler," he said, "you are crazy to go so fast."

Tyler was exhausted. He skied back to the hotel and took a cold shower. His concentration and effort over the last four and one half hours had left him limp.

It was the biggest victory of the season for the Americans. In France, one newspaper devoted a page to the American, Tyler Palmer. In the United States, the press gave him a few paragraphs. Even a paper devoted to ski competition cold-shouldered the event. "Palmer Sweeps Boyne" was the bold headline on the front page of *Ski Racing,* a weekly tabloid, and the article went on to describe how Terry Palmer had won two races in northern Michigan. In another front-page article, with a smaller headline on European racing, the eighth paragraph mentioned that Tyler Palmer had stolen the Lauberhorn slalom from the Europeans in St.-Moritz.

In the late afternoon the sun sets quickly over St.-Moritz. The valley and lake turn a deep blue while the mountains high above turn pink, then a deep magenta and finally they too are deep blue before they hide in the darkness. They are beautiful to watch, beautiful to ski, but they hide their dangers—it was here that Bud Werner and Barbi Henneberger were killed in an avalanche.

The lights flickered on, warming St.-Moritz against night. At the Palace Hotel there was a gracious afternoon tea dance, the traditional rendezvous for après-ski, first stop for an evening of socializing—dinner and a swing at the Grotto Steffani where a light show covered the dancers and walls with color slides that seemed to emulate a collection of pulsating viruses. At Hanselmann's, Mike Lafferty and Eric Poulsen met their two Italian girl-friends, read the Paris edition of the *Herald Tribune,* and ate light pastries filled with fruit, whipped cream and vanilla ice cream dipped in hot, heavy, velvety Swiss chocolate. Scattered on the streets were the carriages of the established St.-Moritz skiers, a huge Cadillac with German plates, an oversized Mercedes with Swiss registration, a Rolls-Royce with a New York license, a Maserati with cross-country skis held firmly in the ski rack. In a penthouse apartment, a wealthy elderly American woman, grey haired, tweedily dressed, speaking excellent French, entertained her friends with a private showing of a ski film and then took them all out to dinner. She had never skied, but had tried the bobsled run at St.-Moritz. In the spring, she would move to her apartment in Paris, or back to New York.

Tyler never visited the town; he spent all his time on the ski hill and in the hotel. He had come to Europe with $3.00 in his pocket and had blown it in Berchtesgaden on chewing gum and post cards.

So is Tyler Palmer, as he withstands his first European press interview.

The road from St. Johann to Badgastein was foggy and the snow was splotched in the valley. Brown earth showed through, and the windshields of the cars were continually mucked by splattered mud and snow. The town rests above the valley. Huge, Victorian hotels encircle the village. For six hundred years Badgastein has been famous for the cure. Take the baths and be healthy again! The water is slightly radioactive and you need a prescription to take a thermal cure. The baths are good for rheumatism, neurologic disorders, circulatory ailments, old age and probably drunkenness too. If your liver is shot, you can get a drink of *bitter Wasser* every afternoon at 4:00 P.M.—2.5 schillings.

"Combine a winter cure with winter sports," says one of Badgastein's brochures. Most of their guests, in January, appeared unable even to fox trot. They were heavy, overweight, they walked about with canes and win-

6. A Bad Scene

dow shopped. The stores displayed expensive jewelry, furs, out-of-style shoes, all with high prices, all seemingly designed for the bourgeoisie who had moved up the ladder, found they had the gout, and wanted to buy something to forget it.

There is a river that flows through Badgastein. Above the village it is dammed, and often there is scum on the surface, but from there the water splashes freely over the rocks and through the village. In the convention building, located in the center of the town, there is a wide stairway that is divided in the middle by a huge marble statue of a thickly torsoed nude woman. She is hefty to look at, succulent, perhaps. Her buttocks are firm, smooth and very cold to touch.

The American team was billeted in Badgastein's most modern hotel, the Elisabethpark. In the afternoon an evening-jacketed combo played ersatz

The main street of Badgastein and the Elisabethpark Hotel.

Lester Lanin tunes to an empty room. Later the furred customers appeared, those that could dance. At the bar were a few Americans, drinking Coke and beer. The potato chips tasted as if they had been soaked in one of the thermal baths, and the bartender whipped out an expensive German or Dutch beer if you did not specify the local product. The people who live in Badgastein seem surly, as if the sickness that visits the town is contagious to the spirit.

Fog and wetness hung in the air as the racers and their coaches inspected the downhill course that twists down the Graukogel. There was good snow at the top and the course was smooth, with good rhythm. It was fun to run. Then, as the trail worked its way into the pine forest, the snow became skimpy. Rocks, some of them jagged, lay bare beside the track. At the bottom, Austrian troops were carrying wicker baskets of snow onto the course to cover a ditch, some bumps and rocks. The racers took one look at the downhill and did not want to run it. One crash into those rocks. . . . The coaches did not like it either, and they and the officials held a meeting. The next day the racers trained again and skis were readied. The race would go on, and the television people arrived and began setting up their equipment. In the Murhaus Hotel one of the Spanish team members was sitting in the hallway looking depressed. "First comes me," he said, "then comes the downhill. I'm not racing!" Hanspeter, acting as head coach while Willy was at one of the women's races, told the team that the downhill race was canceled, there was going to be a slalom, and get out the slalom skis. Tempers were getting a little short. It was still fetid out, and the potato chips seemed to be growing soggier.

Hank Kashiwa has a lot of nervous energy. He is quick-moving, flitting about during the evenings. He wears contact lenses and purple shirts and smiles easily. The non-activity of Badgastein was twitching his nerves with some bad vibrations. He had worked himself up for a race, then it was all taken away. Small things bothered Hank in Europe. Language was a barrier. There were no hamburgers. It was impossible to get his laundry done before he departed for the next race. He could not sleep on trains because he feared he would not get off at the right station. The beds were too small. There was no recognition from the press in the U.S. of the team's efforts. There was no payment for expenses at all, and Hank could not put an extra Coke on his hotel bill—it was not in the U.S.S.A. budget, and neither was his laundry or his shaving cream and razor blades.

There were other problems, bigger ones. Hank began racing in Europe under Bob Beattie, a dynamic coach and promoter who was building a powerful team. Then the U.S.S.A. elected a new president. Beattie resigned and Don Henderson was hired, a nice fellow who did not know his way around Europe. The association cut funds and began comparing amateur racing at home over racing against the Europeans, perhaps for chauvinistic reasons, or perhaps because the Americans never win big against the Europeans. Then, in a political upheaval, the conservative leadership was kicked out; a new regime started to rebuild the racing program. Willy Schaeffler was made coach. He was just the opposite of Henderson, more comparable to Bob Beattie. Hank, who has been coached by all three, felt himself spinning.

More bothersome than the confusing change in coaches, however, was the matter of money—being paid to race, or not being paid.

"I'm riding up one of the lifts with one of the top Swiss downhillers and he tells me that if he wasn't getting paid, he wouldn't get off the lift," said Hank. "I don't have any money and I have to borrow to race. Steve Lathrop is in the same shape. So are Bob Cochran and Tyler. I'm looking to the future. As an American, I'm not allowed to make money racing, and it has cut two, three years off of my career. I fall and I say to myself, What the hell am I doing here, risking my neck? The Europeans ski year-round, and for money, and they got a million people backing them up; somebody is always there to cut a hangnail. If we're paid anything, we're kicked off the team. This system, it's like putting a college football team against the Green Bay Packers. The college team gets killed, you know. I get so damn mad about it I can't even see straight so I put it out of my mind.''

At the beginning of the season Willy decried professionalism. "The motivation is materialistic, not idealistic, and the initiative should not be the green dollar initiative.'' By St.-Moritz, Willy was questioning himself. "The desire has to be there—the total commitment to get up in this sport, and it shouldn't make any difference if he gets three hundred dollars or nothing. But they ought to have something so they can buy a soda pop or get their clothes cleaned. Maybe there is something more. I'm wondering.''

Hank understood Willy. He traded caustic wisecracks with him at times, but he did what Willy said, and he respected him for the organization—travel schedules and hotel accommodations were efficiently arranged for the first time in three years. Hank could put more time on the main problem—racing. "It doesn't matter about your coach so much if you have the desire to win. You got to have it. It's not boring if you're winning.''

Bob Cochran was also a bit anxious with the indecision and inactivity in Badgastein. He shouldered his skis and walked to the gondola lift. He was going to do a bit of free skiing. He had had very little training in the fall, spending most of the time at the University of Vermont, where he is a student. His draft number is 73 and he had to keep up his grades. During the races at Val d'Isère and St.-Moritz he spent many evenings with his books, boning up for a biology exam. It was a dilemma for him. "I'm not ready for school, I want a year to figure it out. I want to race, but if I go to school it is impossible. I see these guys, Duvillard and Russel and the rest of them, they worry about nothing except ski racing. So I have to work a bit harder and get fired up.'' Bob is not sure about his future—maybe he will be a doctor or a farmer, or even a hermit living in the Vermont hills. He does not want a $50,000 house in the suburbs.

Bob and his three sisters, Marilyn, Barbara Ann and Lindy, have the best race training of any of the Americans. Their father, Mickey, bought

Bob Cochran rests after he sprained his ankle . . .

their home in Richmond, Vermont, because there was a big hill behind it. He built a rope tow, and his children and their friends began practicing slalom. During a winter they would run 100,000 gates in their backyard. Then he organized a conditioning program that combined running, calisthenics, isometrics, and isotronics. His children have been racing in Vermont for the past fifteen years, and usually win by several seconds. Some ambitious parents of racers have a strong dose of spite for the winning Cochrans.

Bob took a run down the mountain to loosen up. It was blowing and a light snow was falling as he made short fast turns alongside the course, where the French were also practicing. He did not see the two crossed poles in his path and skied past them into a hidden ditch. His ski tips buried themselves in the snow and he did a flip and lay still. It was a bad spill and the French skiers rushed over and picked him out of the snow. Bob was furious. He had torn the heel plate off the ski and sprained his ankle. He skied quickly down the mountain and the team doctor iced his ankle. That night he lay in his bed with an ace bandage strapping his foot. Around the room lay his luggage, a suitcase cinched closed with a rope, a

bag for his three pairs of ski boots and helmet, a sack full of school books. In the middle of the confusion was a vase of daffodils, given to Bob by a young American girl who was touring Europe and had attached herself to the team.

Bob's sprain was a bad one, and two days later, hobbling on crutches, he boarded a plane for Montreal. He seemed to be happy about going home, but frustrated about racing. He could train under his father, whom he considers the best coach he has ever had, he could study, and perhaps he would be able to race in Maine the next month. But his season was finished.

The word finally came through—no slalom in Badgastein; it will be in Kitzbühel and the downhill will be in Mégève, France. And the racers, who turned out to be in Badgastein for no reason at all, repacked their gear and vacated the town as fast as possible, leaving it to the infirm in their furs and heavy overcoats, to take baths and windowshop, and in the morning to sit in leather padded chairs, reading the newspapers.

. . . And hobbles about the Elisabethpark Hotel.
The injury would bother him for the next six
months.

Kitzbühel," sniffed one middle-aged French journalist, carefully dressed in a dark business suit, *"c'est le bordel de la neige."*

Kitzbühel is alive. It is an old town, compact, with many good shops filled with practical ski clothes. The streets are colorfully lit at night and the architecture, some of it decorated with fancy gold leaf designs, makes you feel you are in Europe. There are lively nightspots. The Kitzbühlers are gay, they smile. Many people come to Kitz just for the après-ski or a little titillation from the Red Devils, the town's resident ski school. And because the race was the prestigious Hahnenkamm, some very important Americans had flown over. From ABC-TV there was Jim McKay, their happy sports announcer, assisted by ex-ski coach Bob Beattie. The two had also covered Val d'Isère, where one of their cameramen had slipped on the girls' slalom course and slid on his can for thirty yards, wiping out about a dozen gates. They had apologized profusely. In Kitzbühel, at the

7. Le Bordel de la Neige

Goldener Greif Hotel, where the American team was staying, the ABC people showed a print of the Val d'Isère race that had appeared on Wide World of Sports. The race, well photographed by Bob Riger's crew, showed a downhiller screaming around a corner and just about creaming himself in the trees. The dialogue was less than scintillating:

MC KAY: ——is going pretty fast here.
BEATTIE: He sure is! He has a good time. He's a top racer!
MC KAY: Look at him on the corner! Gosh! He's made it!
BEATTIE: That was a close one! Looks like he got his weight back.

Next racer:

MC KAY: "Look at him go!"
BEATTIE: "He's sure moving!"

Etc., etc., etc.

Watching the Kitzbühel race is ex-ski coach Bob Beattie, seated on the snow. Leaning on her poles is ex-ski racer Kiki Cutter. The couple is now married.

And there were others from the States—the ski equipment representatives arrived with brief cases in hand, dressed in expensive sport jackets, walking swiftly through the hotel lobby, head up, sure of themselves. They were in Kitz to hustle business, and sometimes they did some extracurricular hustling. They drank, ate and skied on the expense account, and in the evening they discussed why the American team was not winning. They rarely talked to racers; they talked to Willy and tried to arrange things in their fashion, as when one clear-eyed, quick vice-president demanded of Willy that he set up a picture session with the team, as per their contract with the U.S.S.A. The vice-president tried to VIP his way through Willy. It did not work. You never go through Willy. You go under him, around him, over him, agree with him. But you never go through him. Even Tyler Palmer knows that.

Tyler was sitting at the other end of the lobby from the VIPs, drinking something that tasted of orange and had a strawberry in it. He did not have the money to buy it—two girls had paid for it, one brunette, one blond, heavy of face and body. They looked about nineteen. One of the

Pretty, well-dressed girls can be spotted at every international ski race.

girls was rubbing Tyler's knee with her foot, and the other had her hand on his thigh. The brunette whipped out a picture that featured herself in a miniskirt that barely reached to her thighs. "We have to catch a bus at six thirty," she murmured, "there's time." Tyler retreated and took the stairs two at a time to his room.

"You see those girls downstairs!" he said to Mike Lafferty, who was rooming with him. "One wants to go to bed with me so much, she aches all over."

"Hmmmm," answered Laff, combing his hair, "she probably wants to give you a present."

"Yeah," cracked Tyler, "a good dose. Go on down. You'll get . . ."

"Thanks a lot, Tyler," and Laff walked out, laughing. He had something pretty good on the line.

Rick Chaffee walked into the room. "You see those dogs downstairs?" asked Tyler. "Yeah," said Rick, "they propositioned me too." The Austrian chicks go ape over ski racers. Austria goes ape over ski racing. Skiing is Austria's national sport, and ski tourism is one of its biggest businesses.

In a small garret room, Hank Kashiwa was trying to make order out of

Shanny placed poorly, but the Austrian girls still wanted his autograph.

his suitcase. He had just received a "care" package from home: chocolate drop cookies and crackers. Hank had a foldaway bed to sleep on and did not like it. Rogers Little, his roommate, was lying on the bed in his shorts, trying to relax. The Young American Girl from Badgastein was there too. She first attached herself to the American team. Now she was attached to Hank.

Hank Kashiwa unpacks in his room at the Goldener Greif Hotel in Kitzbühel.

Willy had returned from his visit to the women's team and a meeting with Hank Tauber, the women's coach. They were getting some flak. One of the girls had sent to her parents a tape complaining about the rough treatment the team was receiving from Hank. The tape was heard by some officials, who telephoned Willy and Hank across the Atlantic. The girls aren't happy, cool it, was the message. It was a new team, and the girls thought Tauber was riding them too hard, being rough, stern, asking them to do things for no good reason, and in general making their life miserable. Tauber is young looking for his twenty-nine years, handsome and quick witted. Educated in America and Switzerland, he speaks fluent German, Spanish and Romanic. His family is in the leather business, with tanneries in Europe, Africa and America. They also have a vacation estate in Spain. Hank is a good talker, to the point of occasional glibness. He is also efficient and would like to run everything with precision. In some ways, he is an Americanized version of Willy, a person who analyzes problems in black and white, yes and no. He acts much older than his age. Because of his strictness, and also because of his fear of showing favoritism, or perhaps becoming involved with one of the women racers, as has happened several times in the past with other coaches, he had disciplined himself into a stern and cold-minded coach. Too much so, for the girls needed a personal relationship with a coach. It is a very fine distinction that must be made by the coach, and as the season progressed Hank's attitude became more relaxed.

The snow outside was very thin, just enough to cover the slalom hill, which was brownish white. The air was still wet, and morale was not much better than in Badgastein. Poor snow conditions, bleak weather and ski racing distill a potent depressant.

The slalom hill was within walking distance of the center of town, and on Saturday morning streams of spectators followed the racers onto the hill to their annual celebration of the Hahnenkamm slalom. The ritual was the same as always. Red-epauletted police, dressed in grey with automatic pistols in black holsters, regulated the crowd. Chains roped off the slalom hill and the spectators were admitted after they paid 25 schillings. Hawkers set up bulletin boards of picture post cards and photographs of the current ski champions. The spectators climbed up on each side of the hill, about seven thousand of them. Grilled wurst, beer and roasted chestnuts kept the Austrian tummies full. At the base of the course, directly in the center, was a small spectator stand. Here the officials sat—the mayor,

Before and after the Hahnenkamm, hawkers sell souvenirs. Pictures of Karl Schranz are the best sellers in Austria.

the F.I.S. delegate, the ski manufacturers, including Herr Fischer, who arrived in his white private helicopter. The head of Austria's government, Chancellor Bruno Kreisky, had the seat of honor, next to Toni Sailer, a Kitzbühler and one of the super ski racers of this century (three gold medals in the 1956 Olympics). Toni now owns a small hotel in Kitzbühel and is president of the ski club that was sponsoring the race. Toni still has his hair, but his jowls are rounded and his middle is heavy. He is beginning to look like the officials and wives that surrounded him, well fed Austrians moving into the post-prime of life.

Colorful banners flanked the reviewing stand, long rectangular flags that rippled vertically in the breeze. Each one denoted one of the provinces of Austria. From loudspeakers amplified music kept the atmosphere festive—light Viennese waltzes, the oompa-oompa of country bands, then strong, heavy Teutonic march music—a mixture of *Gemütlichkeit* and goose steps. The Austrians do not seem to be quite sure what they are. In Switzerland, race music is conservatively light. In France it is a mixture of

The VIP stand at the bottom of the slalom hill. In the center in the ski jacket is Toni Sailer. On his left is Austria's Chancellor Bruno Kreisky. The unimpressed ski racer walking in front of the celebrity stand is French team member Henri Bréchu, Marilyn Cochran's boy friend.

dance music, love songs, American blues and Nashville. In America, they rarely play music at races.

On a hill overlooking the slalom course was a farmhouse with a balcony decorated with wooden scroll work—gingerbread. A conical haystack stood behind the house and topping the roof was a bell tower with a metal weathervane in the shape of a rooster perched on the peak. A rooster? The symbol of the French ski team?

Because the Hahnenkamm downhill had been canceled, two slalom races were scheduled, the first for fun, the second a World Cup event. The dignitaries were comfortable in their seats for the first race. The TV crews were situated and the race was on. As each racer descended, the quick-tongued announcer rattled off the time from the halfway mark, and whether a racer had fallen or disqualified himself. The spectators were kept well informed. When an Austrian raced, the crowd roared *Op!-Op!-Op!* a much heavier version than the Swiss let out at St.-Moritz. French skiers were awarded very few of the Ops, the Swiss a little more and Gustavo Thoeni, the Italian with an Austrian surname and the fastest rising ski star of the season, received a good number of Ops until he fell. Rick Chaffee made a smooth run and received no Ops.

The Kitzbühel slalom is a tight course because the slopes slant in several directions. Many of the gates are angled into the hill. The slope is quite steep at the top, then drops onto a flat, curves on a side hill, then pitches steeply down to another flat, flows uphill, slides onto another side hill and turns onto the flats to the finish. The course, known as the Hahnenkamm, requires considerable technical skill.

The Austrians, despite the fact that the race was set on a hill where all of them had practiced, could not match the French. Tyler's friend Alain Penz, running number 6, floated loose and quick through the first run with the fastest time. And as often happens, his win boosted his countrymen. Jean-Noël Augert whipped through the course and beat his friend Penz. Then Patrick Russel sped through, squirting his skis, and finished ahead of both his teammates. With three French in the top, the Austrians, even before they started their second run of this first slalom, were demoralized.

Tyler Palmer had watched closely as Augert and Russel skied the course, and he thought that both of them were skiing poorly, even with their taking first and second in the first run. "I can beat them by one sec-

The huge electronic scoreboard at the slalom hill gives the racer's number, and time, broken into 1/100th of a second.

The young Italian racer Gustavo Thoeni, too anxious to win, straddles a gate and goes down heavy.

Thoeni's performance was carefully watched by Jean-Noël Augert. If the Italian stood up, he would have perhaps won. But he fell and Jean-Noël immediately celebrated his victory and mugged for the cameras.

His victory was immediately broadcast and televised throughout Europe.

Even though he was disqualified, Thoeni remained the favorite target of the autograph hunters.

ond," thought Tyler. He was going all out, he wanted to make his position known, that he was not just another American fluke. After his victory at St.-Moritz, Augert and Penz had talked to him about the psychology of winning. Coming in first is a big step up, they said, and the pressure would be heavier because from now on he would be expected to win. Tyler had not fallen in the seven slaloms he had raced in since last spring, and he was confident. He studied the course carefully, then bombed it. After forty sec-

Tyler Palmer in the second slalom at Kitzbühel gets caught by a fallen gate and is tripped to his second spill in two consecutive races.

onds he was one and one half seconds faster than Russel. Eight seconds later, his ski tip hit a slalom gate. The ski split and Tyler fell forward, splattering slalom poles all over the mountain. The spectators who saw him thought he was skiing like a madman, and the press, at this moment, nicknamed him the *Kamikaze*.

On the second run Augert, steady as a stopwatch, finished first, Russel second, Penz third. It was a sad day for Austria. Their best was a seventh.

The team works out in the gym across from their hotel in Kitzbühel. Left to right, Rogers Little, Hank Kashiwa, Rick Chaffee, Hanspeter Rohr, Steve Lathrop, Tyler Palmer. The impromptu volleyball game followed.

It was also a bad day for Willy Schaeffler. Eric Poulsen and Rick Chaffee placed fourteenth and fifteenth, the best American finish. Willy ordered the team to a workout, and at five o'clock, the Americans, clad in their blue running suits, were in a gym located behind their hotel. Hanspeter organized them into loosening up exercises, hopping and jumping. The team was bored with the exercises and, except for Hank and Rick, paid little attention to Hanspeter's directions. Lafferty and Little kicked a volleyball around the court, and it ricocheted from the walls while the gym shook with their yells and laughter. A bunch of high-school kids, Hanspeter thought, they do not take anything seriously. He left the gym demoralized and did not realize that he just witnessed the American way of letting off steam.

A week before, one of the Austrian newspapers had said that the American team was very juvenile in its approach to ski racing. Hanspeter was ashamed, for the team and for himself. "What do I do?" he asked. "Just how can I make them take something seriously?" The Americans do act younger than other racers, and, as a matter of fact, they are, in age and temperament. The Austrians are stolid and quiet and stick to themselves. The French have a good time but they have self-discipline. The Swiss are usually quiet. The Italians laugh and joke among themselves, except Thoeni. He sleeps, eats and skis. "Listen," said Tyler, "the Americans are Americans. The German idea of juvenilism is a little too strict for me—they don't let you have fun, and they seem to be all the same." All these racers, except the Americans, are making a living at ski racing.

That night the latest rumor floated about the press room—the American team was smoking pot. Apparently, it started after the race, perhaps in the mind of a journalist who watched Tyler ski crazily and crash, probably imagining that Tyler would have to be on pot to ski so stupidly. When Hank Kashiwa heard it, he laughed. "And when do we get the time to smoke it, and the cash to buy it? And besides . . ." he shook his head. "Silly."

Most racers do not smoke, some because they cannot afford it, and beer is cheaper and safer, which is what Shanholtzer searched for his first night in Kitzbühel. He went out to a quiet bar and had a beer. Someone, not a team member, spotted him and reported the fact to Willy. Following the first race, with its poor showing by the Americans, and Hanspeter's embarrassing workout, Willy ordered a team meeting in the small television room in the hotel. Everyone appeared, and Willy expressed a few of his opinions.

"You all skied poorly today," he accused them, and then he singled out Tyler Palmer. "Because of St.-Moritz, you are the team leader, and you can pull the team up. You fell, so everybody falls," and Willy went on to berate Tyler by saying his win had gone to his head and that it was ridiculous for Tyler to even keep skiing. By the time Willy was through the whole team was embarrassed for Tyler; Rick Chaffee was blushing. Then Willy lit into Shanny and promised him that he would not get on the A team (Shanny was still on the Training Squad) because of his poor attitude and his breaking training, going out nights and drinking beer. (He was already in trouble with Hanspeter, who had ordered him not to ski beside the slalom course at St.-Moritz. "Why not?" asked Shanny. "Everybody else is doing it." "Because it is the rules," said Hanspeter. Shanny skied down beside the course anyway.)

After the short riot act, Willy read the schedule for the next day—when to appear for breakfast, when to train, and when to go on the slopes to race. Shanny and the other late-seeded slalom racers, Little and Lafferty, thought that their schedule should be later, because otherwise they would have a one-and-a-half-hour wait before their turns. Willy was adamant—everybody up and out at the same time. The racers, a bit steamed, went to the ski room to get their skis in shape for the next day and then went to bed. "Just don't speak to me," warned Shanny, then blurted, "When we win, is it because of Willy, or in spite of him?"

"I knew the chances I was taking," said Tyler, lying in his bed after the meeting. "I make more mistakes than Augert and Russel do, but I wasn't skiing lousy. I'm not skiing lousy if I'm ahead of Russel halfway down the course. Willy should have said I skied well, but I was running too close to the gates. He didn't understand what I wanted to do, and that's to go fast. Hell, I concentrated more today than at any other race. St.-Moritz going to my head, bullshit! Willy is as hard to get through as that," and he tapped the radiator next to his bed.

Tyler was still thinking about the race. He had delaminated his ski tip on the gate. Perhaps he had better move from the gate a bit. What was the trouble, he or the hill? Can he change his speed in the middle of the course, like Augert, and still win? And he was relearning what experience taught him at St.-Moritz—you do not race to beat someone else, you race against yourself.

The French continued their high in the next day's World Cup slalom. Augert again finished first, a feat equivalent to two home runs in a row. He was followed by Penz. Russel and Thoeni were disqualified. An Austrian, Harald Röffner, their best slalomist, finished third, the saving grace for the dignity of Austria and the officials in the reviewing stand. There was talk of firing the coach, of reorganizing the Austrian racing structure, and there was even a rumor that the Austrians were considering a Frenchman for a coach. The fact is, the French are the best slalomists in the world. It has something to do with their training, perhaps because they run so many gates, but also possibly because of the French temperament, so quick and explosive, nervously charged. Slalom is the French racers' favorite event. The Austrians, on the other hand, have always done better in downhill, except when the French, under their talented coach, Honoré Bonnet, developed the aerodynamic "egg" position to increase their speed, studied prejumping, and ordered custom-made nylon suits to cut down wind resistance. The Americans seem to be a paradox. They have the talent and inclination for downhill, yet they succeed more often in slalom. Though not at Kitzbühel. Tyler, Hank and Eric Poulsen were disqualified on a yellow offset gate near the bottom of the course. Hank was furious; he had a good run going. Tyler was somber. He had forgotten, or ignored the advice Dick Dorworth gave him—ski your personality. Tyler had skied the upper course carefully, pussyfooting, and even without the missed gate he knew he would have had a poor time.

The offset gate was difficult; even the skiers who foreran the course had trouble with it. The other racers in the starting gate learned, by warnings received from their radio-equipped trainers, to be careful. The Americans, however, had no radio at the finish line or in the middle of the course, so their races went down unwarned.

Shanholtzer had awakened late, arrived at the top of the slalom course one hour and a half later than Willy ordered, rammed out of the starting gate, caught a tip, and blew the race.

A few hours after the race Augert and Penz were wandering down the streets of Kitzbühel, celebrating their victories, giddy on the local brew. Each was firmly attached to two young girls. The end of the Hahnenkamm race, even with the downhill canceled, was a festive occasion. In the evening the ski school and a mountain band in plumed hats led the ski racers to the front of the school and there, on a platform, Toni Sailer gave a speech, as did a group of other race officials. The band played, the Red Devils ski instructors held lighted torches, gleaming red in the night, and the racers received their trophies, a plate, a wine jug or a special trophy, for first position. The competitors were surrounded by about five hundred spectators, many of them girls who from time to time made a grab for their favorite racer. Tyler showed up in a floppy black cowboy hat with an earring dangling from one ear. Willy arrived in sport jacket and tie. He spotted Tyler. "You think you're some sort of a special clown, don't you?" he said.

Tyler shrugged his shoulders, rolled his eyes, and stuck his hands in his pockets. Augert shrieked, turned to Penz and screeched, "Did you hear that?" and gave Tyler a conspiratorial smile.

Tyler received a Longines stopwatch for winning the Lauberhorn slalom at St.-Moritz. Augert swayed up with that silly grin still plastered to his face, his long hair straggling over his ears, and accepted a large silver

Rick Chaffee receives a trophy from Toni Sailer for his combined standing at St.-Moritz. The racers left St.-Moritz in such a hurry the Swiss had to send the trophies to Kitzbühel for presentation.

chamois, the Hahnenkamm trophy, then retired into the arms of Penz, a steadying, although at that moment not too steady, influence.

Later that night the racers congregated at the Tenne, Kitzbühel's largest dance hall, beer parlor, and pickup joint. Hanspeter was there with his pretty wife, Anna-Luise. Hank Kashiwa was sitting next to Hanspeter, laughing, draped in a roll of red crepe paper that had been thrown about. Firmly attached to him was The Young American Girl, giggling and caressing Hank's neck. In front of them stood a two-liter pitcher of beer. A loud and quite good rock band made conversation pointless.

Eric Poulsen walked into the room as if he were a twenty-year-old Ronald Reagan playing in his first movie. Eric had on a turtleneck sweater and a blue blazer. Neat, with short curly hair, he has the appearance of a playboy. He looked around the room, very suavely, found a table, and took a seat with his girl, a pretty Italian with frizzy hair, glasses, deep brown eyes and a friendly body. He ordered two drinks, then suddenly he was all over the girl, his hands on her hair, then he tickled her, and she broke into uncontrollable giggles.

118

It does not take much to make a ski racer high. By midnight the Tenne was emptied of racers. A few locals remained, as well as a group of American ski tourists who had just flown in on a charter from New York and were busy introducing themselves between gulps of beer. Next morning the racers left for Mégève, for two downhills and a slalom, and the vice-presidents and ski manufacturers and all the other important people left, too. The snow was not that good to ski on, and the American ski tourists spent their first day on the slopes in a fog.

It was the last week in January. There was still insufficient snow in Europe, and the World Cup circuit was half completed. Between them, the men's and girls' teams had traveled some 7,000 miles by train, plane, car and bus, loading and unloading their heavy ski bags, changing hotels two or three times a week. The circuit began to wear heavy for the ski racers who were not doing well, and the frustrations seeped into their conversations as they bickered with each other and with their coaches. Hardly ever could they enjoy the freedom of a downhill run through powder, of meeting new friends, or enjoying a dinner in a small charming restaurant, or of sleeping without a roommate, or with a roommate of their own choice. The Americans, competing in enemy territory, coping with different customs, were uneasy. They were young, and missed home. Some of them had run out of money, and they had very few victories for compensation. They

8. Halfway

were tired, nervous and a bit bored. It seemed to happen this way each year after racing at Kitzbühel. The Europeans, on the other hand, were much cooler about the strain. Their morale was better, because one of their teammates was usually winning, and they seemed to have a facility for amusing themselves in their off moments, a knack that the Americans seemed to lack. The French are inveterate card players, and spend long hours napping and sleeping. The Italians are full of practical jokes, and are buoyant because they like to travel and see the resorts. The circuit is a treat, for most of them are from poor mountain villages, and their town and nation are very proud of their achievements. The Swiss and the Germans and the Austrians keep to themselves, quietly—they sleep, sometimes they play ping-pong. All the Europeans realize that their country has invested much time and money in them, and if they don't win they may be thrown off the team. If they win, they may receive a financial bonus. They are very professional.

The American men fidgeted. Some wanted privacy, away from their coaches and teammates. The high point of the season, their flash of brilliance at St.-Moritz, was just that, a flash. Smiles and happiness. Tyler Palmer with a first, Shanholtzer a fifth, Kashiwa a seventh and ninth, Chaffee an eighth, Lafferty thirteenth—the team placed six racers in the top fifteen of two races. A short, sweet taste of victory, then the heaviness of Badgastein and the two slalom races at Kitzbühel—disqualifications, spills, harangues from Willy Schaeffler about success spoiling the Americans. Hanspeter Rohr remained confused about the Americans who giggled after a disastrous race; he considered resigning, returning to Klosters, his home town in Switzerland, and living in peace with his beautiful wife. Willy was very disgusted. After the last slalom in Kitzbühel he made an acrid, but accurate statement: "Even the Spanish are outskiing us!" The Spanish team consists of two racers, Fernandez Ochoa and Orelio Garcia. They have no coach, and it was not only at Kitzbühel that they outskied the Americans.

The casualties had had an effect. The loss of potential winner Rudd Pyles had been a blow not only to Rudd but to the hopes of Willy and the morale of the team. Rudd could pull things together in his quiet way. The only memory of the injured Pyles was a radio-recorder that the team had purchased for him and were carrying around until they returned to the States and could present it to him. Then in Berchtesgaden, Spider Sabich had quit the team after his confrontation with Willy.

Bob Cochran was another casualty. He had come over with a keen enthusiasm to win in downhill and with only ten days of practice had finished ninth in one race. He certainly had the skill, and perhaps he could do it. But his mind had been bogged down with his draft and school worries, and with a slight uneasiness about the coaches. In the back of his mind he felt that no coach, except his father, could successfully train him. So he relied on himself, and perhaps his self-confidence was not as strong as he pretended it was. After he sprained his ankle in Badgastein, he seemed happy to go home, to rest, to catch up in school, and to train in the backyard with his father helping him. In training there are no losers.

Perhaps the saddest loss, halfway through the season, was Steve Lathrop, a slalom specialist and Tyler Palmer's friend from New Hampshire,

Left to right, Michel Arpin, Head ski technician, Steve Lathrop, Eric Poulsen, and Hank Kashiwa between runs at Kitzbühel. After the race Lathrop returned to the U.S.

a tall, bespectacled boy, twenty years old and quiet, almost too reserved. Steve fell in the Kitzbühel slalom; he also fell or disqualified at St.-Moritz and at most of the other races he entered. The previous season, he had paid his own way to Europe, and in the slalom at the World Championships he had come very close to winning a medal. He had made one small mistake—he had tried to beat the leader, Jean-Noël Augert in a section of the slalom course where he thought the Frenchman was skiing slow. Steve put on the pressure, and he fell at the gate where he had hoped to gain time.

At the beginning of the season, he was the most promising of the young American slalomists. But he could not hold onto it. He was discouraged about racing in Europe against the European super racers. He was discouraged with himself. Willy was riding him hard, trying to force him to do better. Steve was completely demoralized. After Kitzbühel, he flew

Mike Lafferty.

home and his brother met him in Boston. Steve went to Boston Common, sat down on a park bench and spent a half hour in the winter sun, relieved to be home but sad and mad with himself, viciously frustrated because he knew he had the talent to race and to win but could not put it all together.

Pyles, Sabich, Cochran, Lathrop. Six weeks on the circuit and a third of the American team were out, two because of injuries, two because of their heads. "Ski racers are very fragile," said Jean Vuarnet. "I do not know why. Maybe confidence is lacking, or perhaps it is a problem of the young."

Left on the circuit were Palmer, Shanholtzer, Chaffee, Kashiwa, Poulsen, Lafferty, and Little. The last three are all westerners. Eric Poulsen is a tense young man, brought up in a ski racing family where competition is synonymous with victory. Eric was improving quickly in giant slalom. Mike Lafferty, an easygoing twenty-two year old, is a downhiller, and regularly placed thirteenth. In slalom and giant slalom, he was generally poor. After one race, in which he finished in the thirties, he watched the afternoon sunset while nursing a bottle of beer. "It's beautiful here," he said, "the mountains are like this at home . . . wouldn't it be nice to come here in the summer, go for a hike, take a picnic, play tennis . . .sometimes ski racing gets far away."

Rogers Little, from Helena, Montana, a curly haired racer with impish,

Rogers Little memorizing the St.-Moritz down-hill.

sometimes impudent eyes, did poorly in his specialty, downhill, as well as the other events. He seemed lonely on the tour, incapable of expressing himself, though he was quick to observe. At times, Willy intimidated him.

Rick Chaffee had survived five years on the circuit, and he was still strong. After he placed fourth in one race, he gazed at the scoreboard and said to Barbara Ann Cochran, his close friend on the women's squad, "I see it up there, maybe, someday, first . . . second . . . even third."

Rick is quiet, a bit introverted, shy and intelligent. He holds a master's degree in economics from the University of Denver, but he is more interested in politics than statistics. After the Olympics, he plans to quit ski racing and, surprise, not rush into the ski business but go into politics. He would like to run for representative in his home state of Vermont, or work for Senator Muskie—"He's a good man, and I like his stand on environment." Teaching also interests him.

Rick is from Rutland, Vermont. His sister, Suzy, a very good racer, was on the National Ski Team. She is now a model. Both of them started racing early in life, pushed along by their mother. Rick feels a bit dominated by his mother and sister. He does not spend much time at home.

Rick keeps racing because he keeps learning things about himself, things about skiing. During the past season he read a book called *Psycho-Cybernetics,* suggested to him by a Denver kinesiologist, Dr. Marvin Clein, who developed a physical conditioning program for Rick. The book's premise is that positive thinking determines a happy, positive personality, and that negative thinking leads to an unhappy and unhealthy situation.

"I don't think that I am going to embarrass myself in a race, and I do not ask myself what happens if I catch a ski tip. I think about the last time I really skied well and of all the good runs and turns I have made in my life. I think of my goal, that I am going to win a World Cup race. The book is the most encouraging psychological outlook to life I've ever seen! It's saying you can make yourself into whatever you want, and that we are not victims of environment or heredity, we can change it. Now I'm using it in my own life. This is why I keep skiing. I stumble onto these things that I never would have done if I was just going to work and raising a family."

Rick is always searching for the small technical improvements that can make him race faster. He knows they can be acquired. He remembers that Billy Kidd was so poor a downhiller in 1962 that he was pulled out of the World Championship race by Bob Beattie. Bob thought Billy would kill

Willy Schaeffler gives advice to Rick Chaffee and Hank Kashiwa at Kitzbühel. The advice had no apparent effect.

himself. The first time Kidd raced in Kitzbühel, in the downhill, he fell about 120 yards out of the starting gate, going about twenty-five miles an hour. Kidd went on to become one of the best American downhillers. Rick also believes that as a racer you develop as far as your natural ability takes you, and then, to do better, you have to figure out something else. During the season, Rick had been carefully studying the slalom and giant slalom techniques of Thoeni and Russel. Rick was working on one technical point he picked up from Russel—how to plant the ski pole in a position so the skier can accelerate his skis and, at the same time, make a good turn. Rick realized that the pole plant should be done with the downhill shoulder far back and with the arm in front, not to the side. If the arm is too far to the side, then it has to be pulled in to get through the next gate and the movement is less efficient. Small, technical points. Rick was also working on his giant slalom and was learning to shift his weight more quickly from his downhill ski to his uphill ski in a turn, so he could anticipate the next gate.

Rick feels that the American ski racer is a victim of the American ski establishment. "We're playing in somebody else's backyard in Europe, and we're playing against a lot of pros with a lot of depth. We lead a regimented life, a pretty good one, but we're treated like pros, not amateurs—told what to do, where to go, where to race, which skis, poles, bindings and boots we can use, how to dress, when we're supposed to be where; yet we're not being paid to do this, and since it's not a business thing and we're doing it supposedly for the love of sport, why should we be treated like professionals?

"The younger ones on the team really resent this. Then there's that generation gap between the kids and Willy. Everybody wants to think things out for themselves. They act supercool—they feel that the best way to be good in anything is to act like you don't care. There's a narrow distinction between not giving a damn and skiing relaxed. The hippy movement and everything comes out of this deal—you have a whole group of original thinkers who do not want to do what has been done before.

"And this situation over here drains you of the will to win. You start the year and say, 'God, I wish I was in Kitz, racing!' Then when you get to Kitz you don't have that feeling at all. It's a completely different world in Europe on the circuit. And also back home you have factions in the U.S.S.A. fighting for power. Some are coddling you and some are pissed at you, trying to get you to quit because you're too old or something. It is really hard to take when you're not doing it for business. Why make ski racing my life if I can't make a living at it?"

Two years ago Rick wrote his master's thesis on the market potential for K2 skis on the East Coast. The Washington state ski manufacturer liked the thesis and paid him $2,000. The deal was approved through the U.S.S.A. Then the new regime came into office and told him he was ineligible to race. Rick returned the money in order to hold onto his amateur status.

"I wonder what they would have done," mused Rick, "if I had given the money to my parents for what they spent on me when I was racing as a youngster?"

The women's squad was also having problems. Traditionally, they have always skied the international circuit with more flair than the men, and ever since 1948, when Gretchen Fraser won an Olympic gold medal, there

Rick Chaffee shares a happy moment with Barbara Ann Cochran. They are good friends and Rick often visits the Cochran home in Vermont.

have been American female champions. Gretchen was followed by the Vermonter, Andrea Mead, who won two gold medals in the 1952 Olympics, and by Betsy Snite, Penny Pitou, and Jean Saubert, who also garnered medals. Recently the American girls have been particularly strong. In 1968 Marilyn Cochran was the world champion in giant slalom. Her sister Barbara Ann won a second place in slalom in the 1970 World Championships while Marilyn took third place in the combined. Two women on the previous season's squad, Kiki Cutter and Judy Nagel, were consistent winners, but at the end of the '69–'70 season, they retired from racing. It just was not fun for them anymore; there was too little compensation. (Was it really $20,000 that the French girl racer, Michèle Jacot, earned for winning the World Cup?) Besides, they were "getting involved," falling in love, and their favorite coaches had also resigned. In the present season, Marilyn and Barbara Ann Cochran, Bob's two older sisters, were the only remnants of a once powerful American squad.

"I can always count on Barbara Ann or Marilyn to finish in the top five," Hank Tauber said at the beginning of the season, "but people in the U.S. don't understand; they think only of wins. There are many admirable finishes in the top ten."

Marilyn and Barbara Ann were not racing as well as expected. Marilyn, a big-boned girl, almost always smiling, at twenty, a year older than her sister, skis with tremendous power. She looks rough on the course, but she is very fast. Talented in giant slalom and slalom, she is beginning to break through in downhill. She is the senior member of the women's team, as is Rick Chaffee on the men's squad. Marilyn's winter had been fairly consistent. She and her sister were not "on their skis" in giant slalom; their timing was off. In slalom Marilyn would invariably run the first course hard and place within the top three. On the second course she would attack, wanting desperately to win, but would catch a tip, or miss a gate, or fall and disqualify. She did it in six races during the season, getting up from her spill and skiing off the course, sobbing in loud gasps of anguish. Marilyn cries a lot. She cries when she falls and she cries when she wins. Her morale was low during the first part of the season and it did not help her sister, Barbara Ann, who was also disqualifying.

"Why do I do it?" Marilyn moaned. "I know it's in my head. The first run I ski the way I can, but then, when I have a fast first run, I feel I have to go faster to win the second race, and I guess I just don't have the confidence to do it.

"There's a lot of pressure on me and Barbara Ann," she added. "A lot is now on our shoulders because Kiki and Judy quit. Racing with them helped our morale. And I'm so erratic, you know. I'm sick of reading in the press how lousy last year was and how good this year is going to be. They expect so much from us and then if we don't come through, they get pretty negative."

Marilyn has been on the National Team for three years, and in that time, like Hank Kashiwa, she has been trained by three coaches. In her first year there was Chuck Ferries, a young ex-racer who was technically good but, for Marilyn, was much better as a psychologist. He knew how to get the girls up for races, what to say and when to say it. But then he and the rest of the Beattie staff resigned under menace of new political powers

Marilyn Cochran after one of her spills during the second slalom run. She will regain her breath, cry out her frustration, and ski off the hill.

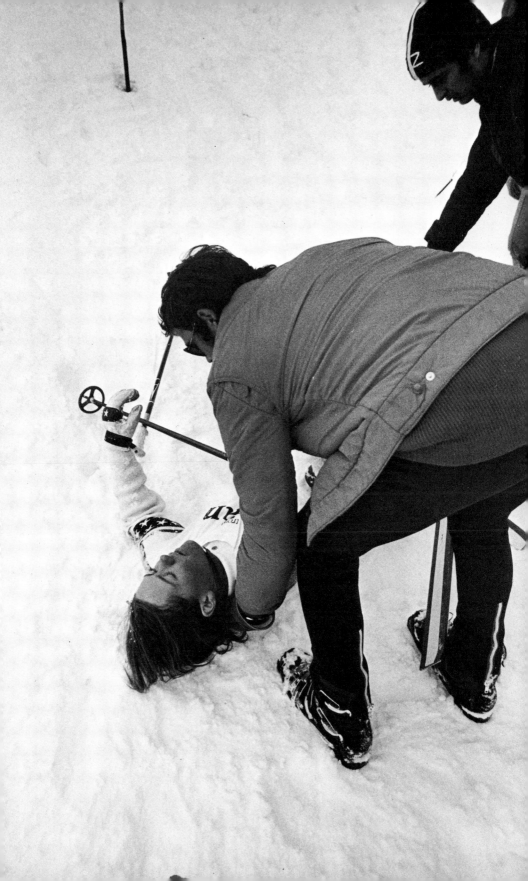

in the U.S.S.A., and Dennis Agee, an easygoing coach from California, replaced him. He lasted one year. Although the new coach, Hank Tauber, tried not to play favorites, he was fond of Marilyn and tried a number of tricks to make her relax and finish a second slalom run and win. He used anger, exasperation, persuasion, soft soap, eagerness, forget-it-all. In the end, he would say nothing. Marilyn's father, Mickey, wrote her one letter while she was in Europe. The main point, he stated, was to concentrate— do not let things bother you. It was the same point that Tyler Palmer was learning. Marilyn was being too introspective. She could not mentally block the first run out of her mind when she was running the second courses. Concentrate only on what you are doing is the cardinal rule of the slalomist—forget the first run, your time, and your closest competitor.

"You know, I wonder why I do race," mused Marilyn. "I guess a lot is wanting to be the best in something, the best in the world, and that's what we're trying to do in ski racing. Racing is enjoyment for me, and you meet interesting people." In Marilyn's first year of international competition, three years ago, she wore her hair short and frowned a lot. She was a bit detached from the team, slightly shy. Marilyn was still in high school, where she played in the school band and was a straight-A student. She did not go out with boys much. This season her hair was longer and her cheeks were rosy and she was relaxed. She has a smile for everybody, including Henri Bréchu, a member of the French team who is one of her closer friends. She is learning to speak French with him. She was looking forward to the race at Mégève, when the girls and boys would be together for the first time since Val d'Isère. She was desperately hoping to stand up in the second run in the slalom and cry from winning, not falling.

While the Americans were losing racers, the strong French women's team added a sixteen and a seventeen year old to their squad, Danièle Debernard and Jocelyne Perillat. It was an official, glorious affair. The French Minister of Sport and the French Federation officials, plus the coaches and the women's and men's teams gathered together in St.-Gervais, and the two teen-agers were awarded the team sweater with the *coq*— the symbol of the French team—sewn onto it. It would be one of the most memorable moments of their racing careers. The awarding of the *coq* is what all young French racers aspire to, and it is difficult to achieve. It is a symbol of pride, status and success.

The American girls were coming to Mégève from southern France, where they had raced in a downhill. They had had fresh snow there, done some free skiing and looked forward to seeing the men. The men were happily leaving Austria, hoping that the change in countries would improve their morale. The oppression that had moved into the men's team at Badgastein was proving a difficult virus to shake.

The '69–'70 slalom champion, French racer Ingrid Lafforgue, broke her leg at the beginning of the season. So her sister, Britt, took her place and became the '70–'71 slalom champion, tied with the Canadian Betsy Clifford. Ingrid rebroke the leg during the summer of '71 and her ski career may well be finished. She is twenty-three.

The fastest route to Mégève from Kitzbühel is through Italy. You drive over the Brenner Pass, where Hannibal, elephants and troops passed a dozen centuries ago. He traveled free. Now it is two dollars per car, with a stop at the Italian customs where they ask you politely if you have any cigarettes and you answer that you have no hash, thank you, and then the road snakes through Bolzano and Trento, across the Adige River. The Adige appears to be the garbage dump for all of northern Italy. You drive onto the Autostrada, flick past Milano and curl up the mountain to the Mont Blanc tunnel where, if you are not lucky, a French gendarme with a tight little moustache will flag you down at the dividing point between his country and Italy and fine you twenty francs because, as a good driver, you put your headlights on. One should not do that in French tunnels. One should put one's dimmers on—parking lights only. You pay and

9. Griping in Mégève

thank him profusely for welcoming you into France and hope that an avalanche from the mountain above falls on his head.

It is difficult to understand the French. They are Latin people who rely on emotion, individualism and intuition, which is never wrong. They like to eat and to make love and to talk about it and, at their leisure, perhaps do a bit of work. If a person works too hard, is ambitious, assumes a managerial position and tells people what to do, he is a "fascist." The French people govern themselves on the basis of mutual distrust, one experienced journalist has stated. The French are like the can openers they use, bright, shiny instruments, intricate in design with a place for oil. They do not function at all as you would expect.

Generalities are only generally true, and the mountain people, as in every country, are a breed apart. They are friendly, open, and at peace with themselves. It is a compromise they make with the rugged and beautiful mountains they live in. The French are, for all their internal combustion, a likeable people, and the American and the French ski racers are good friends. They have much in common.

Now they, the Italians, Swiss, Austrians, even a few Russian skiers, were in Mégève. Just down the road, in St.-Gervais, were the girl racers. Snow had finally fallen, but the St.-Gervais women's downhill had been run at Pra-Loup, six hours distant, the Hahnenkamm downhill for men was set for Mégève, the Mégève slalom for men was rescheduled for St.-Gervais and, surprise, the Mégève downhill (Coupe Emile Allais) would be run at Mégève and the St.-Gervais slalom for women would be held at St.-Gervais.

"What a queer town," said Shanny. "I went out to run a bit and immediately got lost. I had to retrace my steps. Then I took another run and again got lost! I never get lost!"

Mégève is picturesque. The streets meander aimlessly, narrow streets that are better for walking than for driving. Everybody walks and gazes at

Mégève is also well known for its sleigh rides, although the racers were provided free transportation by Hertz.

the shop windows. People come in all types in Mégève: the wealthy, families, good-looking young people, even the *petits chats,* as the Savoyards call them, the men with the ankle-long fur coats and the very narrow shoulders. They can usually be found at Les Enfants Terribles, a small club with mural walls by Cocteau and a white and gold gilded cherub floating overhead. The place smells of Johnson's Baby Powder. There are other clubs—the Viking, with an uproarious English rock band whose sound is somewhere between the Beatles and the Rolling Stones, and L'Esquinade for the older crowd.

The Hotel du Parc is a large, squat family hotel. Most of the residents seem to be non-skiers, pasty-faced middle-aged types who prefer to sun themselves and go for sleigh rides. This was the American team's hotel, and when they arrived they were surprised to be greeted by—we will call her Mimi. Mimi is famous. She has blond hair and blue eyes and small, well-formed lips that she keeps wetting with a sharp, pointed tongue. She identified herself to the hotel as the interpreter. Mimi has been interpreting for the racers for years. She has interpreted for the French team, the Italian team, the Swiss team and even the Norwegian team. She is a veteran, she is, but now Mimi is a bit older, and she devotes most of her time to interpreting only for the French and American teams.

"I don't mind girls chasing around," stated Willy, "but they ain't staying in the same hotel. That's final." Well, it was not always final.

The Young American Girl, the one who had attached herself to Hank, checked into a nearby hotel. A few ski reps also arrived, including some friends of Michel Arpin, the Head Ski representative who also acted as unofficial coach. He is a former French team racer and when Killy was winning, Michel looked after his equipment.

They were all sitting in the lobby, drinking coffee and Cokes. It was the end of a day of training and Hank Kashiwa was fidgeting. The Young American Girl came in and sat down, all smiles, with fresh green makeup on her eyes. She looked like a puppy dog. Mimi joined the group and coyly pinched Hank's ear. Hank reached over and gave Mimi's hair a playful tug. The Young American Girl leaned over and whispered into Hank's ear. They both left the hotel. Mimi went into a deep discussion with Michel Arpin.

The next day fresh snow was falling; it was cold, foggy and windy. A Vermont type of wind, brutal and gusty, blew most of the powder from the

John Hollow videotapes the men's downhill at Mégève.

downhill track. It was another day of training, and four French coaches were on the course, each with radio and stopwatch to time the skiers on different sections of the course. John Hollow, the American team manager, was videotaping a tricky S curve. Below the curve Willy timed the skiers on the flat. Eric Poulsen skied past wearing a nylon wind shirt that rattled like a luffing sail. Willy shouted into the radio to the start, where a K2 representative was filling in as starting coach, "Tell Eric when he comes up to fix his damn goggles, ya, once and for all, and take off that silly parka he's got on and put on his number! He has a low line and is making a lot of noise and skiing on his inside ski. Stay on the outside ski, all the way, and in every single turn!"

Something is always going wrong with Eric in downhill; his goggles fog up, or there is a loose strap someplace. He looks out of place on a downhill course, and he does not like it.

That night the team watched the video playback. Rogers Little made a fault in a turn and Willy had the sequence of the mistake replayed three times. Rogers was having a bad season, missing his line and making tactical mistakes. After the show Rogers, practically in tears, complained to Willy that he never gave praise, or a kind word.

Rogers' best finish this season was twenty-three. He was another American who could not pull it all together, yet he had been brought up on skis. Rogers was first on the National Team during the '69–'70 season and had a fairly good year winning a few American races and placing well in some World Cup events. Over the previous summer he had trained hard and had looked forward to the race season. Then he could not find himself, perhaps because he had spent the summer in a school, making up courses in economics. He needed only a few more hours to complete a degree and he was contemplating law school. He found it difficult to race, to devote a life to it; he planned to quit after the Olympics. He had observed the European racers, who had nothing but racing to live for, and he did not like the future prospects, although he appreciated the prestige of being within the one percent of American racers who compete in Europe.

Rogers' father, Dr. Bud Little, is the United States representative to the F.I.S. He attends the annual international congress and other meetings and fusses about ski politics. So it caused quite a bit of consternation at Mégève when a Swiss photographer pinpointed Rogers as the recipient of an under-the-table payment (about two hundred dollars) from the Nordica boot company. This is strictly against the U.S.S.A.'s rules and if Rogers had received the money, he would have been automatically kicked off the team and the Nordica boot company would have been banned as an official supplier to the U.S. Ski Team.

A Swiss newspaper first brought out the charge, saying the Americans

Willy Schaeffler times Eric Poulsen's downhill run.

Michel Bozon's grave in Chamonix. He is the third of the Bozon family to be killed in the mountains during this century.

were taking under-the-table payments, but not naming Rogers. Willy wrote the newspaper and told them he would sue unless they retracted the charge. They did, but then the photographer pinpointed Rogers. Libel proceedings were initiated against the newspaper. Most of the team members, when they heard of this "scandal," laughed. "Pay off Rogers?" said Shanny. "Why, he hasn't done a thing all year!"

The day of the first downhill race turned out clear and the course was crisp on top, a little soft on the bottom section. The top third was above treeline; then it curved into the woods, through an S turn, and into a meadow. There were many flats on the run. It would be a race for a *glisseur*. The better racers grumbled. The course was too easy. Last year it had not been easy—in the middle of the woods, the trail had made a short turn and pitched quickly into what was called *le mur de Borne*. It was bumpy, and the line the skiers raced was on a steep traverse. Many have missed

140

this line and fallen. The course had been very icy the previous winter, and in training the racers felt fear; it became their main aim to finish the race in one piece. One skier did not. On the *mur de Borne* Michel Bozon, a young French racer, fell. His speed carried him off the trail and he hit a post, put there to protect the skiers from going into the woods. He died in a few hours from internal injuries.

The death of this young skier from Chamonix caused the formation of what could be called a racer's union. Under the leadership of Franz Vogler, Germany's best downhiller, the racers pressured officials to make downhill races safer. The Mégève downhill was completely changed. The *mur de Borne* was abandoned and the new trail took a semicircle around the dangerous section. Many downhill aficionados protested, fearing a wholesale evisceration of the famous downhill trails. So far, the surgery has taken place only at Mégève and St.-Moritz.

The Mégève course was indeed too easy for many of the downhillers, and the technical skiers, such as Schranz and Duvillard, the ones who know how to handle speed and difficult turns, were disgruntled. "I am happy for France," said Duvillard. "They now have three more kilometers of autoroute."

The Mégève downhill.

The most technically demanding part of the course was the S turn. There were a few sections in the forest where the trail was quite narrow, and what appeared to be heavy-duty volleyball netting was strung beside the trail. If any skier should fall and shoot off the course, the netting would prevent him from crashing into trees. Two men were assigned to the net. They spent the race drinking wine. Every so often, a skier blasted over the edge at about fifty miles an hour and *whap!*—he was entangled in the net, a fly in a spider's web. The two men—by the end of the race they were quite happy—stumbled out from under the trees and extricated the racers, who were happy for the protection, even while feeling a bit sheepish. Vogler, the racer who initiated the change in this downhill, fell into the nets at the exact spot where the new section of the downhill began.

Willy had left the hotel at seven o'clock and had ridden the tram to the course. He was worried about the snow and the waxing of the skis. It had snowed the day before, a light powder, but during the night the snow had stopped and the temperature now was rising. That could change the snow from light powder to a wet texture, as heavy as mashed potatoes. With a small snow thermometer Willy measured the temperature of the snow, then the air, and radioed the figures to Hanspeter at the hotel. Through charts supplied by the wax manufacturers and on the basis of his own experience, Hanspeter waxed the skis of the racers just before they left for the course. Today he waxed for a slightly warmer snow temperature, and the racers put strips of paper between their skis before they carried them up to the tram car. The paper would protect the wax applications on the two skis from sticking together. As the race began, Willy moved down the course to the tricky S curve and, with his radio, remained in contact with Hanspeter, now with the racers at the start.

With the warmer weather large crowds had gathered at the finish and the S curve, waiting for some spills. Willy watched the first-seeded racers carve through the S turn; there were no Americans within the first fifteen, and Willy saw now that the race would be strictly for *glisseurs.* It was apparent in the S turn. The Swiss skiers, much of whose training during the summer had involved free skiing on their glaciers, glided through the turn, riding high and sliding their skis very little. So did Malcolm Milne, the Australian, who was not doing as well this year as last; he was skiing with an injured back. The first American to come through was Mike Lafferty.

*Spectators gather at a dangerous bump in hopes of
seeing a disastrous crash.*

Mégève features some chic racer chasers.

He headed into the turn too abruptly but lost little speed. Shanholtzer held a good line coming into the turn but slid his skis coming into the flat and never recovered his speed. Little, Poulsen and Kashiwa made small technical errors that gave them poor times. For Willy, it was a disappointing race. The Swiss finished in the top position, followed closely by the French and Austrians. Mike Lafferty had finished ninth, his best of the season, but Willy was dissatisfied.

During his years of college ski coaching, Willy's team was practically always in first; he ran an efficient organization. Now he was putting in fourteen-hour days, scheduling the team's day, going to jury and coach meetings, officiating at races, worrying about the budget and where they would stay at the next race, and always trying to instill in his racers that gritty feeling of attacking, of competing to win. The downhill race at Mégève was, to him, a frustrating anticlimax to three days of training.

Coaches never have an easy life, even those who run the powerful European teams. Two years ago the French team members signed a petition to have their head coach, René Sulpice, removed from his position. He was replaced by Jean Béranger. The Austrian Ski Federation, the government, and the ski manufacturing tycoons were after Professor Hopplicher, the Austrian head coach, because his only big winner has been Karl Schranz, and Schranz is not very friendly with Hopplicher. Urs Weber, the Swiss coach, resigned after the close of the successful 1970–71 season because he did not want to be a tool of the Swiss Ski Federation. Jean Vuarnet receives the most vile and threatening letters from the relatives of the Italian girls on his team. If their daughter is violated, if she comes home no longer a virgin . . . Betsy Clifford is at war with the Canadian coach. And so on.

Coaches get together from time to time, over a bottle of wine—Willy likes burgundy—and they too bitch, about their job, about racers, about their organization.

WILLY: I didn't know that our racers were so far down the hole until I came here, how much we have lost. But if you let the racers decide when to train, you don't need a coach anymore. Send their father and mother over instead.

HANSPETER: In the U.S.A. parents push their kids, and the kids feel it— that they are racing because of their parents—and then they turn around and say no, we're not racing anymore. Kids have much more to say in the U.S. and the parents give them everything. If you say no, the kids run away, or I don't know what.

WILLY: The kids and the parents think the world owes them a living. Our kids giggle and laugh more than the others. They're younger acting than the Europeans. They have a different philosophy—do what they want to do. I think it's basically something they learn at home. In Europe, kids don't have a baby sitter. Kids when they're six and seven stay at home alone all night—they have responsibility. Mother isn't looking out for the little ones, as she does in the United States until

A racer in the narrow section of the course.

Shanholtzer held his line well in the difficult sections of both Mégève races only to lose it on the easier flat section.

they're eighteen—"Watch out, Charley. . . . Don't do that, Charley . . . !" When I was eleven or twelve I had more responsibility than some of the team members now have.

HANK TAUBER: The whole development program in the States is very bad for downhill. You get no help from the areas—they will run a giant slalom instead. They're afraid of downhill and their parents are afraid. The French, they put up these hairy downhills and they say there is the start and finish. Go!

WILLY: College is a cop-out. If a racer doesn't do well he leans on his education. A lot of kids are satisfied to make the National Team but do not have the will to go all the way. I ask them, what do you want to be, satisfied and happy and go through the season and have a good time, or do you want to fight to win? The team was completely deflated during last season.

HANSPETER: If a European was on the American team, he wouldn't say much, he would just leave, because there is no money.

WILLY: We don't know where we stand. Is ski racing going to be an Olympic sport where everything is amateur, or is it going to be the World Cup where people advertise the wins? The way it is now, it cannot go on.

HANK: We take a lot of crap from the people in the States. They call me a jerk for taking somebody to Europe to race, and I just take it. I'm not putting up with politics, and I'm sure Willy isn't either. Willy is older, so they come to me and give me a rough time.

WILLY: There are only about ten qualified coaches in the States, and most use the job as a jumping board for publicity. We have no coaching clinics.

HANSPETER: Sometimes, I just cannot comprehend how the Americans think. What do they really care about?

HANK: You can wax their skis ten times and the skis run well and you don't get a thank you. But you miss it once and you get hell fast. This is particularly true with the Americans. Whatever it is, it is the coach's fault.

WILLY: This circuit has an unbelievable schedule. We live like gypsies. We don't have one day to relax or sleep in. Coaches feel the same way the racers do. We'd love to go out with the team and find some powder snow and enjoy it like everybody else. But there isn't time.

HANK: Willy is in an impossible situation. Everyone back home thinks he is going to wipe everyone off the map, that he is going to say five magic words and the kids are going to win. This is absurd. You need a good foundation, dedication. It will take a few years.

WILLY: Why do you do it, coaching? A few wins are far more appreciated

150

and all the headaches are fogotten. There is a greatness to bringing it out in a racer, a reward that cannot be measured in dollars. Any other coach would say to hell with these creeps. You need a helluva thrust to stick with it. But two or three ups are good enough. They eliminate the downs.

The bottle of wine was empty.

The Grand Hotel du Parc at Mégève has a typical three-star European hotel dining room. It is large and rectangular, painted in white. Long windows with light-colored drapes keep the room bright and airy during the day. There is a large chandelier and under it, in the center of the room, is a white-clothed table covered with platters of hors d'oeuvres, fresh country cheese, tarts, usually apple and cherry, and cream-filled pastries. The dining room tables surround this centerpiece; each is neatly covered in white linen. On the tables are bottles of mineral water and wine, some of them half empty, the remains from the last meal. Dinner napkins are neatly tucked into small napkin rings.

The food is sustaining. There is a large choice of hors d'oeuvres—saucissons, pâté, tomatoes, salads of shredded vegetables, sardines, cucumbers. There usually is a soup, a broth as clear as day and practically as tasteless,

10. "This Can't Keep Up"

or a strong country potage that is excellent. The main course will be chicken, with a cream sauce, or veal, with a gravy sauce. Occasionally there is a steak, green beans and french fried potatoes. For French cuisine, it could be considered a hearty meal—good but rather blandly put together. Compared to American hotel fare, it is superb.

The American team's table was long, big enough to seat the racers, Willy, Hanspeter and his wife, the team doctor and his wife. A small American flag and some flowers decorated the centerpiece. There was mineral water on the table, Evian or Perrier, which is bubbly, a bottle of wine, to be consumed by the coaches and the doctor and his wife—wine also was not in the U.S.S.A. budget. The team drank mostly apple juice and Perrier.

Dinner for the Americans was at seven thirty, a little early by French standards. The team members appeared singly or in twos, took their seats and had their plates filled by the white-coated waiters, deftly slipping the food onto their plates with a fork and spoon. Willy is a good dresser. His favorite sports jacket is a light-weight brown houndstooth that fits him beautifully. He wears well-cut cord pants, and Gucci shoes adorn his feet. He is handsome and suave in these clothes, which he wears for dinners not only at Mégève but also in Washington, Hyannis or Sun Valley when he dines with Ethel Kennedy and a collection of young Kennedys.

Willy expected the team to dress for dinner. Well, at least to have the team sweater on. Conversation was quiet. Tyler walked into the room. He dipped his mop of russet colored hair to the black-coated maître d'hotel, who returned a bow. Tyler had on a short-sleeved shirt. For Tyler, it was fairly plain, a drab, soon-forgotten solid color, with an open collar. The short-sleeved shirt blew Willy's mind. Tyler also had on a crazy-looking belt that some chick had given him, and it was holding up a pair of jeans disguised as black pants. Tyler wasn't wearing any socks and, well, that sort of did Willy in. Later in the lobby they had it out.

"You want a shirt, I give you one!" Willy said.

Tyler did not like the way he said it—a bit sarcastic—and he sassed him right back. Willy responded with a quick remark and things got out of hand. They started yelling at each other. A heated rage burst into Tyler's chest and surged into his head. He curled his fists and was ready to nail Willy, but caught himself just before the explosion. He popped out of his chair and started to lope to his upstairs room. "Don't you walk away from me!" Willy yelled after him. Tyler whipped around. "You want to talk to me, Willy, you talk to me in my room!"

When Tyler was younger and locked into a rage, he would punch his hand through the wall, any wall, and scream to himself. You can see it in his hazel eyes that crackle and his chin that can jut out as far as a rattlesnake's head. Tyler has a wild Irish temper—mother's side. He was furious now and ripped into his room, slammed the door and paced about, mumbling and swearing to himself. Then he ripped off his clothes—his shoes, pants, underwear and that short-sleeved shirt—threw them on the floor and yanked open the door to the balcony. Snow had drifted deeply onto the porch, and Tyler, nude as a Yankee farmer taking a skinny dip, plunged onto the porch, squatted deep into a snowbank, and glowered at the dark trees waving in the wind and the warm glow of Mégève. It was

The TV room of the Hotel du Parc at Mégève. The team is watching videotape playbacks of the day's downhill training.

dark that night, cloudy, but every so often the stars gleamed through. A strong wind was blowing up. Tyler remained still, hunched over like some cornered animal, and let the snow burn, then cool his back, buttocks, thighs, and feet. He remained in the snowbank for ten minutes, until his feverish head cooled down and he began to shiver.

Then he whipped back into his room, put on his clothes, including the short-sleeved shirt, and packed his bags. He skipped downstairs to have it out with Willy. If it did not go well, he was splitting for New Hampshire. Willy was not there. Tyler returned to his room but did not sleep well that night.

Tyler was not entered in the Hahnenkamm that was scheduled to run in Mégève the next day. Willy was on the course early. For the Swiss, it was a beautiful race; they again took two of the first three positions, but for the Americans it was a disaster. Lafferty fell in the flat a few hundred yards from the finish. The snow was soft and Laff dug in a ski and broke it. Kashiwa, Little and Poulsen placed poorly. Shanny blew a critical turn before a three-quarter mile flat to the finish. He lost his speed and had no chance to place well. He knew it at the finish line. He unsnapped his helmet, dropped it to the ground, dropped his poles, and when he found the knots on his racing bib could not be undone easily, he ripped the number off and walked through the finish area to the scoreboard mumbling to himself.

Willy was furious with his team and called another meeting. It took place in the hotel's TV room, which was plushly carpeted and had a marble fireplace decorating one wall. Heavy curtains kept out the light. Willy, Hanspeter and Hank Tauber were there, and the team settled around them. Willy stood up. His face was red, and as the meeting progressed it turned scarlet.

"I am ashamed to be coach of the American team!" he snapped. "You looked horrible, and you raced horribly! Lafferty, for you to fall on the flats is stupid. It is childish." Then he berated him for his long hair (which he had cut in Kitzbühel), before switching his attention to Tyler.

"Tyler, you look a disgrace," and Willy criticized him for his poor skiing since St.-Moritz. Then Willy started in on the short-sleeved shirt.

"How come you don't wear your team sweater?"

"I'll tell you in private," answered Tyler.

"You tell it to me here, it's just the team."

"Tauber is here."

"Tauber is part of the team."

"I don't like Tauber."

Tauber remained quiet. Hanspeter was carefully studying his hands. Then Shanny walked in, late as usual. Willy was on him in a flash.

"You! You don't care about racing and cooperating with the team and

Mike Lafferty getting a trim in Kitzbühel.

your attitude at the finishing line was terrible. I want to kick you off the team because of your foul mouth and bad attitude!"

Shanny was flabbergasted. "Willy . . . what's going on?"

"Ya, you know what's going on! . . ." and Willy informed him that the profanity he had shouted at the finish line had been picked up by the TV sound men, who played it back to Willy, and also showed a tape of Shanny throwing his helmet and ripping off his number.

"Oh, my God," muttered Shanny, and he pieced it together. After he had taken off his helmet and dropped his poles and the number, he had walked across the finish area, about forty feet from anybody. "I'm sure it didn't look very good, but it really wasn't that bad, and I was walking across the finish area, and telling myself in very unfriendly terms about what I thought of my run, and one of those TV sound guys must have had a directional mike, and it probably sounds like I'm screaming."

"Well, what did you say to yourself?"

"I think I said, 'Oh God! You sure fucked that one up!' "

As Willy raved on, the team started giggling. Lafferty gave Willy a small bye-bye wave with the hand. Willy retorted that there would be a bye-bye for the whole team. Palmer laughed. Willy started after him. "Sure, Willy," he replied, laughing sardonically. It was bad.

Willy was due to leave with Hank Kashiwa for Sapporo, Japan, by way of Geneva, Denver, and San Francisco not long after the meeting. There was a pre-Olympic race—a tryout of the courses. Willy was going to inspect the facilities and Hank would represent the National Team in the races. Willy was feeling a bit grey.

Tyler cornered him alone and apologized, as well as Tyler can, for laughing at the meeting. "We were just trying to keep our sanity," Tyler explained, and then he told Willy that Lafferty was fed up and, really, he had had a fairly good season, and it was better for Shanny to throw things than not care at all, and that Tyler himself wasn't doing that badly.

"This can't keep up," said Tyler. His bags were still packed. "Or I'm leaving, and I want a definite answer, yes or no, are things changing?" Willy agreed, as much as Willy can ever agree after such a personal confrontation. Then it came out about the short-sleeved shirt. Over Christmas, Tyler was completely without funds. So were his parents, and it looked like a thin holiday. Tyler wanted to give his father a present, but with no cash . . . so he gave him the American Ski Team's official train-

After the Mégève meeting. Racers prepare to depart.

ing sweater, blue and red, with stars on the shoulder. It was a handsome sweater, and it was what the team members, except Tyler, wore for training and to dinner.

The races were over and Willy, wasted by the emotion of the meeting, had packed his bags and loaded them into the black Mercedes he had been lent for the winter. Hank Kashiwa came out with his ski bag and strapped it to the car rack. When they drove out the circular driveway, only Mimi, the pretty blonde, remained on the hotel porch. The rest of the team were in the hotel.

The two months during which the young racers had lived and trained under their new coach had convinced them he was an autocratic disciplinarian. They called Willy a heavy-handed Kraut. What few of them realized was that Willy, like them, had started his life as an avid skier who disliked authority, discipline, regimentation, and the draft. During World War II, Willy's rebellion against the political-military establishment in Germany nearly cost him his life half a dozen times.

Willy was raised in Bavaria, not far from Garmisch, where he learned to ski. His father was a Social Democrat, and since Hitler was not very well disposed to political opponents in the mid-thirties, the father was placed on the blacklist. Willy was drafted in 1937, and in a letter to an uncle in Chicago he described some of his training. The letter was censored. Then the government extended his Army duty, two weeks before he was to be discharged. Just as any modern American youth would do, Willy bitched, loud and clear. The Army brought forth the letter and accused Willy of being a spy. They criticized him for lack of patriotism. As Willy was not in the Party, and his family was blacklisted, they busted him from warrant officer to private and sent him to the Dutch border to what was called a baby concentration camp. For the next year and a half he dug ditches from 5:00 A.M. until 4:00 in the afternoon. He was twenty-one, the same age as most of the racers he now coaches.

Willy was released in 1938 and started to live a happy period as a test driver for the Ford Motor Company. On weekends and holidays he was a Garmisch ski instructor. When the war broke out, his presence on the blacklist saved him from being drafted. But the Army reconsidered in 1941 and inducted him into the ranks as part of a penal battalion. The battalion was sent to Poland to build bridges. When the offensive into Russia began, Willy's penal battalion was offered a chance to rehabilitate itself. The men were given weapons and were used as special patrols and on spearhead missions. Willy was somewhere behind Moscow, as part of a pincer movement, when the temperature dropped to −54 degrees and the Russians began to pull the Germans apart. Willy put on the clothes of dead Russians. He was captured and lined up before a firing squad. He went through a very quick and intense period of concentration, where his life flashed in an instant. They fired and Willy, sure he was dead, fell to the ground. The Russians, drunk on vodka, fell down too, laughing madly over their practical joke. Willy managed to escape and rejoin the Germans. His life on the Russian front was probably saved by his fifth wound, shrapnel in the right lung and upper heart chamber. He was evacuated in a plane, which was shot down behind enemy lines. Willy, one of two survivors, hid in a small compartment for two days before he was rescued. He was transferred from one hospital to another until he arrived in Munich, weighing 130 pounds. It was 1944.

The military establishment decided that Willy, after he gained twenty pounds, was so well trained in winter warfare that he could rehabilitate himself again by returning to the Russian front. Willy silently refused. At about the same time, American Flying Fortresses blasted Munich. The headquarters building was evacuated before the raid but Willy and a friend lingered and filled a knapsack with code numbers, passes, stamps, requisition orders. The building was demolished by bombs five minutes after Willy rifled the offices. A day later, Willy and his friend were dug out of a nearby bomb shelter. No one would ever know that the papers were stolen. Willy split for Austria.

He could, with the papers, go anywhere, requisition guns and munitions, food and uniforms. He entered the underground, harassing the German Army with sabotage. His biggest coup was in 1944, when Hitler ordered a last stand at St. Anton. Tanks, cannons and supplies were brought in by train from Germany through the Arlberg Tunnel, and the guns were being dug into the lower slopes of St. Anton—where today there are ski slopes. Willy blew up the tunnel with a box of dynamite and for the rest of the winter, from his hideout on the Valluga mountain, watched German troops struggle over the Arlberg Pass.

After the war Willy fished out a few top Nazis who were hiding in Austria and managed to land his old job at Garmisch, ski instructing American troops. One of his students was General George C. Patton. They became friends and Patton helped Willy, who had been living for two years on forged identifications, to receive official papers and the goodwill of the U.S. military.

World War II is history; the emotions of that period are lost on the younger generation. Yet pehaps it is the residue of that period of hardship that has forged this particular generation gap, the difference between the easygoing young American ski racers and the older, German-born, adopted American. Willy developed, in his younger days in Bavaria, as an independent thinker who believed in self-determination and who loved to ski. His beliefs, and they were as strong as are the anti-Vietnam war protests of the youth today, turned him into a rebel against authority, the establishment, draft, right-wingers. He developed his own philosophy, survived against the odds, and became a person who dislikes criticism, and who is uncompromising in his beliefs. When he was twenty-one, the average age of the American ski racer, he was, because of his independent, outspoken attitude, digging ditches in a concentration camp. In fact Willy, a German who sabotaged the war effort of his own country, has all the qualities that the young Americans think are so cool. The difference is that Willy was nearly killed a number of times because he adhered to what he thought was correct. Discipline and physical stamina and the will to win, or survive—that which he hopes to instill in his young American skiers—kept him alive. Money, prestige, security were luxuries he never knew in his youth.

11.

Willy Schaeffler and Hank Kashiwa were in Sapporo, Japan, racing and making suggestions for improving the race trails for the Olympics. Mégève was a memory. For the first time that season, Willy was able to analyze himself and his relationship with the team.

Little and Shanholtzer had also left after Mégève to race in the United States, and the remnants of the American Ski Team—Lafferty, Poulsen, Palmer, Chaffee and their assistant coach Hanspeter Rohr—drove from Mégève to Crans-Montana, Switzerland, for a giant slalom race that, because of lack of snow, replaced the Kandahar downhill. It was an easy race, relaxed, and Eric Poulsen finished fourth, behind Duvillard and Thoeni. Mike Lafferty was happy, for he was seeing the friendly Italian girl, whose daddy happened to own a chalet in town. It was a short stay of two days, and a few hours after the race the competitors drove down the

Tyler Breaks the Barrier

winding road that snaked past the vineyards into the valley of Valais. Within a few hours they arrived in the Lauterbrunnen valley and parked their car next to the Schilthorn Tram, more popularly known as 007, for the tram car was an important prop in the James Bond movie, *On Her Majesty's Secret Service.* The tram lifted them 2,400 feet to the town of Mürren, the setting for the Kandahar slalom and their last race of the season in the Alps.

Mürren is a small, isolated village built into a promontory overlooking the Lauterbrunnen valley. There are no cars in Mürren, which gives the town an extraordinarily tranquil quality. This peaceful village is surrounded by one of the most memorable views in Europe. The Eiger, Jungfrau and Breithorn, three of the most awesome mountains in the Bernese Oberland, encircle the town. On clear days these and other mountains

A lone racer skis to the start of the giant slalom at Crans-Montana.

The slalom hill above Mürren. The mountain is the Jungfrau.

The 007 cable car that lifts skiers from the valley floor to Mürren and high-altitude skiing.

sparkle under the sun, and one can see six glaciers, masses of snow and ice that fold down the mountains' sides as smoothly as spilled syrup. The mountains are beautiful in their frightening immensity, yet they are comforting, perhaps because they, so huge, are mute and still, and you, so small, are alive. Mürren and its setting is one of the jewels of the European Alps. The English have known this for years and it is their favorite ski resort. Here is the winter residence of the Britisher who founded modern ski competition, Sir Arnold Lunn. Sir Arnold, who climbed most of these mountains in his youth, is famed for inventing slalom racing and in 1928 initiating, with the late Hannes Schneider, the Arlberg-Kandahar, first held at St. Anton, Austria. The race is a descendant of the Roberts of Kandahar race, a downhill first run at Crans, Switzerland on January 7, 1911. The winner, Cecil Hopkinson, won over nine other competitors in sixty-one minutes and Lord Roberts presented him with a trophy. It was the beginning of Alpine skiing.

Sir Arnold—his intimates call him Arnie—is old, his body worn and tired. He is eighty-four. His eyes are hidden behind thick glasses but they sparkle brightly, blue as the sky, and his mind is as crisp as the mountain air. As the father of Alpine racing, he is not happy about the Olympic Committee's Avery Brundage wanting to remove the top World Cup competitors from the Olympics because they are paid to race.

"I did not start this game as a professional sport. I wanted amateur sport. But the race times have speeded up, and the racers are competing for their countries and they now train ten months a year. No modern man can give up ten months of a year to train unless he tends to become a professional. The Olympics are to compete, not to win, but it is now important to win because it is a career for life.

"The present situation with the Olympics [The Olympic oath requires that the participants do not make money in the sport in which they compete. It is signed by each competitor.] is causing young people to commit perjury. A soldier is a man brave enough to die for his country and an Olympic amateur is a man brave enough to lie for his country.

"Brundage, I know the old boy. He is the last remaining Victorian snob. A Victorian snob is very rich, likes sports; he is something like a gentle-

Sir Arnold Lunn receives a trophy at the Palace Hotel for his long years of service to skiing and to the Arlberg-Kandahar Club.

man. I am 100 percent for corrupt amateurism. I am disgusted with a sport in which young people are taught to lie."

Sir Arnold's apartment looks out on the Jungfrau and Eiger, and in the morning, if it is warm, he will sit on his terrace, dressed in a bathrobe. He enjoys a touch of whiskey. On his desks are scrapbooks that go deep into the past of Sir Arnold and the Kandahar Club. On one page there is a picture of the skiers who attended one of the earliest of the annual dinners, in 1926, at the Palace. The men, dressed in white tie and tails, tall and elegant with short hair slicked tight to the head as was the custom of the period, stand beside their chairs. The women, seated, are in long evening gowns. The setting at the table is elegant and the picture exudes an aura of formal graciousness. Below the photograph is a typewritten letter from the manager of the hotel to the secretary of the Kandahar Club. The manager apologizes for the fact that the hors d'oeuvres were not satisfactory the year before and promises to rectify the fact for the next dinner. On the bottom of the letter, written in hand, is a postscript: "Caviar is sixty francs a kilogram."

Tyler Palmer had never eaten caviar and vaguely knew that Sir Arnold Lunn was the originator of slalom skiing, the event which Tyler was dedicating his life to. The young Yankee's mind was locked into the immediate

Tyler Palmer, center, hones the edges of his skis before the Mürren slalom.

Tyler in the starting gate . . .   . . . And Jean-Noël Augert.

and practical problem of how he was going to race through the combination of gates set on a steep hill overlooking Mürren. It was a clear day, sharp as pain, and the course was hard. Tyler still was not sure whether he could pull off another win, and he studied the course carefully.

Tyler's victory three weeks previously in St.-Moritz had done nothing for his racing appearance. He still tied his race number in a tangle around his middle, his shirt tail was out, and his ski pants were rumpled in confusion around his ankles, where he had pushed them above his ski boots. Ahh, but the ski pants were new, blue ones, skin tight. They were not the Bogner pants that had been promised him in St.-Moritz, but a pair given to him by Alain Penz, one of his pals on the French team. Penz and Augert looked after their poor American friend.

169

After Tyler had sidestepped to the top of the course, he pocketed into his subconscious the mental image of the run he would make and with a small metal file sharpened the edges of his skis. He was running tenth; the new F.I.S. points were released and Tyler, because of his victory at St.-Moritz and his fourth at Berchtesgaden, was ranked fourth in the world standings in slalom.

Thirty seconds before the start, Tyler placed himself in the gate, glanced down the course, spit, and planted his poles. His face was impassive as last-minute thoughts flicked through his mind—stay loose, attack, keep on the outside of the gate, go for the gate, attack to the finish line. Go like hell. He went like hell, and the Kamikaze finished the first run with the best time, 11/100ths of a second ahead of Augert—about half a ski length. Tyler sidestepped up the second course with Augert; his friend was the only threat to victory. They came to a flush, four gates set on a flat before the last pitch to the finish. "Watch out here," Tyler said to Augert, "too much speed here, and a racer would not make the gate."

Forty yards farther up the course, Tyler turned to Augert. "I'm going to take it fast. How about you?" Augert did not say anything for a while, then answered, "Me too." Rosko is his nickname and he is tall, angular, and has hair down below his collar. It hangs straight, limp, the color of hay that has been in the barn too long. Rosko is loose physically and mentally. He lives for three things: ski racing, motorcycle riding and listening to rock music. He is crazy about rock and would like to have his own band or a discothèque. Last summer he had the chance to hear a Rolling Stones concert, and he flipped. He says he loves America because there you can wear your hair long and dress casually; it is good lifestyle and nobody cares. In the fall, Rosko will go bird hunting, dressed in his Colorado leather cowboy hat and leather jacket. He always has a smile on his face, except when he is racing, and then his rather large, hooked nose and serious mouth give him a slightly voracious hawklike appearance. Rosko is very aggressive, and he was determined to snatch victory away from Tyler.

In the second run, Tyler was the fifth racer on the course, Rosko was running fourteenth. The advantage was to the Frenchman. If Tyler fell or had a poor time, Rosko would be under less pressure and could cool the race. In any case, Tyler had to run the course all out, but he knew that anyway. He had learned at Kitzbühel that he could never again pussyfoot down a slalom hill.

Jean-Noël and Tyler study the course before their second run.

Tyler was still an enigma to the press and spectators, and again they expected the Kamikaze to explode. He disappointed them, skiing with control, and finished strong, beating the nearest rival, Patrick Russel, by slightly less than two seconds. It was an overwhelming victory, except that Rosko had not yet made his second run. Tyler had programmed the first run out of his mind, and also Rosko's time. Tyler knew how hard it was to

On the course, Tyler Palmer in white, Jean-Noël in black.

be in first place on the first run and to pull out another first on the second run. But now he wanted to beat his pal so much he was grinding his teeth. He waited at the finish line, looking up the hill, watching for Rosko.

Nobody can turn on speed within a slalom course like Jean-Noël Augert. He ran the course all-out, sitting back, then squirting his speed, slithering through the gates, and beat his friend by half a second. It was an unbelievable run and Rosko had just won his fourth straight slalom. He was exhausted when Tyler congratulated him. He smiled wildly and told Tyler, "You are crazy to go so fast."

Tyler also was tired from the pressure, and back in the hotel he took a cold shower and lay down on his bed. He went over the race in his mind. He had made two mistakes, one at the top and the other at the flush he had warned Rosko about.

Still, Tyler was satisfied and felt good. The race had proven to him that he was in the same class as the best in the world. He had learned what it took at Kitzbühel and put it together at Mürren. There was a very fine difference in how he skied in the two races. He had cooled his runs at Mürren, not by slowing his speed but by controlling his state of mind. He had learned the limits of his ability and how to operate within them. "I'd snake ahead, you know, trying to make a tenth of a second, and I found it wasn't worth it. I know what I can do now. It's all tied together by this race.

"You know, I wasn't quite sure at St.-Moritz, and I was apprehensive at St.-Gervais, but now I expect myself to be up there. Fourth doesn't seem a good place to me now—first, second or third—it depends. Not fourth. I never dreamed of being this good this year, skiing as well as Augert and Russel. I didn't know what it took; now I know—just go like hell."

Tyler had gotten it, he had broken that barrier into the first three, and he was not about to vacate the premises. Rick Chaffee came in fourth at Mürren. He was having one of his best years, but he had not cracked the barrier during his fifth year of racing.

Tyler now had another goal and that was to surpass Augert. He had to learn how to adapt in the middle of the course, how to change speeds, set a clock in his head so he could mentally time each portion and adapt his body to the read-out. He wanted to beat the long-haired Augert, his best friend on the circuit, so much that it hurt. He was becoming that exception to the rule—an American champion.

The Arlberg-Kandahar event is always celebrated with a huge banquet

The banquet room of the Palace Hotel.

and this year, as in many years past, the celebration took place in the venerable Palace Hotel, the meeting place for generations of Kandahar Ski Clubbers. The hotel is more Victorian English than old Swiss. Potted palms and poinsettia hide in the corners and fake Persian rugs of the best quality are on the floor, in design and signs of wear much like the old rugs of the Chantarella at St.-Moritz. They are comfortable in their aged look and make the guests feel at home. In the lobby a large glass case holds ancient trophies. "Keep 'em pointed downhill!" is inscribed on one of them, a silver ski. The hotel has a huge banquet room and that evening it was filled with racers, the press, club men, and the younger set, mostly English. There was a rock band that played to a light show, but most people remained seated at the long tables that run the length of the fifty-foot room. The Martini International Club (liquor distributors and importers) sponsored the affair and served trays of orange juice and gin, Scotch neat, and wine glasses of dark Martini vermouth, which hardly anyone drank. The English drank the orange juice and the gin, the press stuck to the Scotch, and the Swiss mixed the Scotch and the orange juice. Several Swiss started yodeling, a sure sign that they had reached their limit.

The slalom at Mürren had been a relaxed affair, for the most part. Eric Poulsen had come very close to placing second in the Kandahar combined, but he had disqualified in the second run of the slalom. The night before, the American team and the other racers had attended a party. Mike Lafferty had stayed a bit later than the others, dancing, and left with a loose, happy smile. The next morning he had disqualified in the slalom, as he had in the giant slalom at Crans-Montana. At the finish line, Hanspeter came up to talk to him and Lafferty leaned over his poles, his head almost touching Hanspeter, and quietly cried and whispered that he just could not put it together, he just did not know how to do it. Hanspeter gave him an easy hug and told him just as quietly that the race was finished, keep working at it, there is always the next race, your downhill is good. A small boy came up and took Lafferty's bib, and as Mike left the finish circle a number of young girls and boys surrounded him and asked for autographs. A smile came back on his face as he signed.

Malcolm Milne skied through the finish and came to a stop next to Hanspeter. He had also disqualified on his second run. "You had a good thing going, with your first run," said a friend, "too bad you messed it up."

Malcolm flashed his smile. "Yeah, didn't I! I'm getting there!" and he walked up to Hanspeter's wife and gave her a friendly hug. He had been working on his slalom all year, and it was improving. It was a satisfying season for Malcolm even though his downhill was suffering because of his back. His main problem at Mürren was trying to find enough money to fly to America and race there.

The bib snatchers. Every race has boys at the bottom of the course to retrieve the bibs. Racers like to keep them for souvenirs but the clubs who sponsor the race and pay for the bibs do not approve of the custom.

In the dining room of the Palace Hotel. Tyler Palmer, left, mugs with Hanspeter's wife, while Hanspeter pays attention to the sliced lamb.

Without Willy, the team was more relaxed, the dinners in the Palace Hotel less formal. Yet of the team that remained, all the racers except Lafferty—Palmer, Chaffee and Poulsen—maintained a keen desire to win, and a strong self-discipline. Laff, brown eyed, soft smiling, an easygoing Westerner, attractive to the girls, seemed to lack incentive and direction. It bothered him.

On a bright afternoon, while most of the English tourists were napping, the Americans loaded their skis and gear into an electric cart and followed the cart and the porter to the 007 tram, which lowered them to the valley. It was the first week in February and the next competiton would be 4,000 miles away, in Canada. The Americans were relieved to be going home, and the Europeans were excited about their overseas trip.

Sir Arnold was happy to see the racers leave. Before the men had come to Mürren, the women had raced there and Sir Arnold was perplexed about the rising costs of sponsoring a World Cup race. He had estimated the cost of the Kandahar at 20,000 pounds sterling and believed the price would be prohibitive without the help of TV. "You know," he said, "there is a declining class of skiers who pay their hotel bills, and people who do pay their hotel bills should have races organized for them. I think we should reorganize the Duke of Kent races. It was a race for fun and in a small race, you shan't get any money."

On Sunday evening after the slalom, the only racer left in town was Malcolm Milne. He was drinking beer in the Palace, trying to hustle a young English girl. The next morning he was gone.

12.

The World Cup and Tall Timber Classic at Sugarloaf, Maine! Yessireee, folks, the biggest, most glamorous, most exciting shindig we ever did put on! Come see the daring Europeans defy death on skis! Come see the prettiest girls in the ski world! Come see . . .

Sugarloaf worked hard on the biggest winter event in Maine's history. Started in August they did, planning. Spent about $80,000 in cash and time. They are enthusiastic up there, down east. Set up a hospital with two doctors and a bunch on call. Had the National Guard send in a helicopter big enough to transport the Swiss and French team, and their coaches, to the nearest hospital. A private company sent in their helicopter too, a skinny little thing. Arctic Cat lent fifteen snowmobiles and volunteer drivers hoisted the press to the finish line—wouldn't do to make them huff and puff. Five trailer vans were set up for the skiers to care for their boards

Down East Spectacular

(that's what they call skis in Maine). One hundred ski patrolmen volunteered to police the race course. The State Police were in force and if your car did not have a pass—park down the road a couple of miles and take a bus to the resort. The State of Maine sent a truckload of lobsters, clams, corn on the cob and one chopped-up moose for a big clambake. Each member of the press was given a duffle bag filled with thirty-five pounds of Maine-made goodies and propaganda—a bottle of Poland Springs mineral water, canned sardines, maple syrup, pre-mixed old fashioneds, a wastepaper basket full of brochures and, among other things, a roll of toilet paper.

For the opening ceremonies three eighty-foot white pine poles were set in front of the base lodge, with the mountain as a backdrop. The Maine Maritime Band played the National Anthem and nostalgic, Saturday af-

ternoon Sousa and bandstand rhythms, and on signal three bearded lumberjacks decked in red and black lumberjack jackets raced up the poles and fixed on the flag of Maine, the flag of the United States and the flag of the Fédération Internationale de Ski. They rappelled down in one swift descent. "Ohhh!" went the crowd. The foreign racers were awe-struck. Some show!

"How come they climb trees?" asked Malcolm Milne. Somewhere he had found the money to make the trip.

"Because they're lumberjacks."

"What's a lumberjack?"

"They cut down trees for a living. There're lots of trees in Maine."

"Well, why don't they cut them off at the bottom?"

Then three F-101 jets swept over the mountain in what is known as The Missing Man Formation. The middle jet dipped the stick, lit the afterburner and arched out of formation, straight up, and disappeared into the blue sky—in memory of the missing and dead in Vietnam. It was very touching and disconcerting. What the hell are we doing, ski racing and eating lobsters and moose meat while guys are killing and getting killed?

No matter, the show must go on and everybody was there. Governor Curtis of Maine was there. The president of the F.I.S., Marc Hodler, was there. He flew in from Switzerland. Stein Eriksen, the beautiful ski instructor from Aspen, was there. The famous ABC crew of McKay and Beattie were there, acting wet and chagrined when it snowed—what's Maine compared to Kitzbühel and Val d'Isère? Even the public announcer for the races was imported—from Colorado. He told everybody over the PA system that he was Warren Miller, a well-known ski filmmaker. Actually, he is Steve Knowlton, and the resemblance between the two is fairly remarkable, because they are both bald in the same way. Knowlton rarely gave the times when he announced the race, just pitterpatter—"He's a good racer, and here he comes to the finish line and let's all give him a good hand! . . . OOOps! He Markered out . . . unnnh, I mean, well, he could have *Salomoned* out, or *Tyroliaed* out, or *Looked* out." Knowlton belonged to the glamorous Tenth Mountain Division—he will not let you forget it—which was recruited during World War II, consisting only of serious skiers (an unglamorous part of their story is that many of

Lumberjacks rappel down the flag poles erected at Sugarloaf, Maine. They had just put up the flag of Maine, the American flag, and the F.I.S. flag.

Two of the lumberjacks with a Candahar gal.

them were blown to bits with their mules in the muck of Italy). They are now the "old-time skiers," and *Marker out* was one of the postwar, early ski era expressions of what happened to a skier when he fell—his German Marker bindings released him from the skis, and he cartwheeled down the slopes. Marker was the first safety binding to be marketed in the U.S., but as the sport of skiing became popular, and commercial, Marker was followed by Look, Tyrolia, Salomon, and other ski equipment manufacturers. The representatives of all these companies were at Sugarloaf, hustling. Steve "Warren Miller" Knowlton did not want to offend any of the hustlers.

Overnight, posters and stickers were plastered on lift shacks, cars, buildings, skis. "Hexcelerate" said one, pushing a new ski called Hexcel. A big poster proclaiming Head, in orange and black, was tacked above the lift-ticket office. Small Lange stickers were passed out. Spalding, Rossignol, Fischer, Dynamic, K2, Olin, Raichle, Henke, all of them had their salesmen hustling, attending cocktail parties and acting the big happy time.

"Out there you need us, Baby," "This is Bonne Bell Country," warned bumper stickers. Bonne Bell is an American company that manufactures lip and skin ointments for the ski market. They give fancy cocktail parties and have a bunch of girls pushing their products—all of them are good skiers and they dress in bright, tight ski pants or star-speckled Liberty Bell (yeah, a subsidiary) warm-up pants and jackets; they smile prettily and pass out small red, white and blue tubes of the stuff. They are the Bonne Bell Barbie Dolls—dress them in a different outfit everyday, wind them up and send them out to glamor up the race—a group of girls as cosmetic as Amyl para-Dimethylamin-benzoate, a tube of which they might hand you if you were to meet one. With a big smile of course. They have competition. The Candahar gals tout a European ski ointment and they are dressed in red and wear head bands and smile and have the stuff they are promoting smirched over their lips. Fem Lib has not yet hit the ski circles.

The downhill course, which would be raced four times, was beautifully prepared. It was also heavily policed. The course was roped off and National Ski Patrolmen, in their rust-colored parkas, were the guards. They allowed officials on the course, including the gate keepers' and officials' families, all identified by yellow armbands. Ex-racer and ex-National ski coach Gordi Eaton, who had helped set the course, was not allowed on to inspect it. Photographers, except the TV people, were forbidden to venture on the downhill to find a suitable spot to photograph. As a consequence, there was poor picture coverage and the course guards were referred to as the Maine Gestapo and Brown Shirts. Even Karl Schranz had trouble. When he went up the course to train, one of the National Ski Patrolmen would not let him on. Schranz just looked at him in amazement, then anger. "You motherfucker!" he bellowed, and skied through him and down the course. Schranz speaks English quite well.

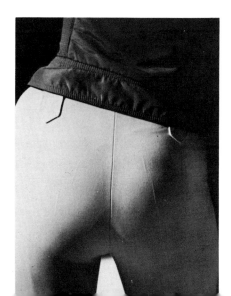

Rear view of a well-fitted spectator.

*Willy Schaeffler, sick from exhaustion and a collision, sleeps in a base-
ment bunkroom at Sugarloaf.*

Willy Schaeffler and Hank Kashiwa had returned from Japan, after a
twenty-two-hour trip, and Willy, fatigued but surprisingly relaxed, greeted
Hanspeter and his team briefly at the Capricorn, where they were staying.
Somehow, no reservation had been made for Willy, and he ended in a
bunkroom in a different lodge. On his first day in Sugarloaf, Willy inspected the downhill. The guards let him on—he was wearing half the
American flag on his uniform. Then, as he was standing on the course, one
of the yellow arm-banded sons of a yellow arm-banded official careened
down the race trail and hit Willy from the rear; it was a high-speed clip
that pole-axed Willy into a lump on the snow. Willy spent the rest of the
race in his basement bunkroom, drinking hot tea mixed with honey and

The finish of the Sugarloaf downhill.

lemon, and suffering from a slight concussion, lung congestion and exhaustion. He kept in touch with the team through his portable Motorola.

The Sugarloaf downhill suffers from the American malady of flatness. Eastern mountains do not have the terrain to match the speed, steepness and danger of the famous downhills of Val d'Isère, Kitzbühel and Wengen. The Sugarloaf course is a long, sloping flat with two long-radius turns and a few bumps. It is merely a good course for the *glisseur,* but to the down east spectators it was a spectacular course. They arrived early, some 8,000 of them, and trudged up the sides of the trail. Many carried on their backs wicker pack baskets filled with sandwiches, soup, hot coffee and wine. The women wore floppy parkas of conservative, New England colors. The sporty, outdoorsy men wore knickers and smoked pipes. Most of the spectators were slightly pasty faced, the by-product of sub-zero days and nights spent in overheated homes, eating too many canned vegetables and enriched bread. When the racers flicked by, they ohed and ahed again, and sometimes gasped. "Lookee there Maw, lookit'm go! Gosh almighty." They were shocked and thrilled by the speed, and they were delighted with the colorful tight-fitting suits the racers wore. The spectators were happy; they did not have to pay to watch the race. In Europe, the sponsors of the race would have been $8,000 richer.

"You watch," said Hank Kashiwa in Kitzbühel, "the American team will really be up for the races in the States."

In Maine, Hank was so fatigued from his Japanese trip that he could not "get on" his skis, and for the rest of the season he would be off. The momentum that he had built up in Europe was lost. The girls, though, were up. In the first World Cup race in America, up in Quebec, Marilyn Cochran and her sister Barbara Ann had finally put it together and finished 1–2 in the slalom. At Sugarloaf, five American girls finished in the first fifteen in the downhill.

The American men could not match this victory. Bob Cochran, who had been home recuperating from the ankle he injured at Badgastein, still felt pain, but he was well enough to race at Sugarloaf. He held high hopes of placing well and retaining his low starting position for the Olympics; these were the last World Cup downhills of the season. He finished seventeenth in the first downhill, eleventh in the second. He was furious with himself at the finish line. While his father, Mickey, quietly talked to him, Bob punched his ski poles viciously in the snow and with his fist beat himself on the thigh, pounding it over and over. He was sliding on his turns and losing speed on the flats. His lack of training in the fall—two weeks—constituted the biggest gap in his struggle toward a first. With adequate training he would have had more confidence and perhaps he would not have hurt himself. So in Maine he beat his fist onto his thigh, aching to wear a hair shirt. Hanspeter never did understand Bob, who never wanted advice on the downhill course; Bob always wanted to figure the course out for himself.

Rudd Pyles made it back, too. His jaw was healed and his back, although still sore, could sustain the pressure of a downhill. In his first race he finished twenty-ninth, in the second fourteenth. He was happy. "It gives me the greatest confidence in the world to be behind these racers by only one and a half seconds after being on skis for only three days." Rudd had been off skis for two months and the race had proven that he still possessed the aggressiveness and drive that it takes to run a downhill. Some downhillers, after a bad crash, lose their courage and desire. Rudd, who calls himself a good loser, was encouraged, and at the finish he was calm and reflective, as a downhiller should be. Bob Cochran, beating his thigh, was displaying the personality of a slalomist.

"You're skiing marvelously," Willy commented to Steve Lathrop, who had also rejoined the team. Steve was shocked to hear Willy praise him. Willy's caustic, critical tongue was one of the factors that had driven Steve into a depression in Europe. Praise from Willy gave Steve an uplift, and starting fifty-seventh in one downhill he finished twenty-second.

"Are things going to change?" had been Tyler's question in Mégève. Now Willy, although sick and flat on his back, was pleasant with the young skiers, and he and Tyler were becoming friends, or at least forming as close a friendship as there can be between a twenty-year-old ski racer and his fifty-four-year-old coach. Willy was trying—he had even brought

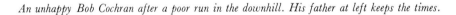

An unhappy Bob Cochran after a poor run in the downhill. His father at left keeps the times.

back a complicated chronograph-stopwatch from Japan to present to Tyler.

Willy had also eased his authority by promoting Hanspeter to men's coach. The promotion meant that the day-to-day training of the National Team would be under Hanspeter, while Willy would be spending more time developing the junior program in the United States and setting up coaching clinics. "Aw, Hanspeter," one team member said in Badgastein, "he's under Willy's thumb. He can't do anything." None of the team members had realized that Willy, since the beginning of the season, had planned on turning over the coaching responsibility to Hanspeter as soon as his assistant was familiar with the team, budgets and planning.

Willy's thoughts on amateurism versus professionalism had also changed. He had come to realize that the serious ski competitor, racing in the World Cup circuit, must either be wealthy or have financial support. "I'm not supporting amateurism," stated Willy, "I am supporting the rule I am working for, which is the U.S.S.A. Myself, I would work for a golden middle way, where the association pays the team members—so much for racing, so much for training."

Willy was upset that the racers had to pay for their Cokes, laundry and day-to-day expenses. He was trying to raise money for them. The team heard about Willy's efforts but they did not believe they would be compensated. The U.S.S.A., they felt, was not at all concerned about the racer's financial position, only that the racer should not profit. "The U.S.S.A. is run more like an extortion racket than a ski federation," was the comment of one European official, when he heard of the financial hardships of Tyler Palmer and the Cochrans. (Yet by the end of the season the U.S.S.A. reimbursed each female on the national team approximately $80.00 and each male $200.00.)

There were still problems, though, particularly with Shanholtzer. Shanny had left the team after the Mégève event and had raced in two back-to-back downhills in Steamboat Springs, Colorado, and aced both of them. "It was one of my better experiences," recalled Shanny. "I stepped in the starting gate and I was sure that I was going to win. I knew I was going to ski as well as I was capable of, and no one was better."

"What if Russi, Cordin and Duvillard had been there?"

"Well," Shanny shrugged his shoulders. "I would have had another race. I'm not in their class. Yet."

After these races he picked up an airline ticket from the U.S.S.A. and flew to Boston, then caught a ride to Sugarloaf. When he walked into the Capricorn lodge everyone was surprised to see him—Hanspeter, his team-mates, the race technicians.

There had been a rumor, and as soon as Shanny heard it it became apparent to him that Willy's attitude might have changed toward the team, but not toward him. Shanny was not supposed to be in Maine, so the story went, because Willy, before he went to Japan, had canceled his airline ticket from Denver to Boston. Shanny, through a mix-up in the Denver office of the U.S.S.A., had received the "canceled" ticket and, not knowing of the circumstances, showed up in Maine. Even Willy, according to Shanny, was surprised to see him. "Where were you?" said Willy. "We even called the postmaster in Jackson Hole, trying to locate you."

Shanny did not believe him. If anyone had tried to find him in Jackson Hole, they would have. Shanny was there and knew everyone in town. "He told me in Mégève," Shanny said, "that I would be racing in Maine. Then he canceled my ticket." Shanny soon heard that Willy had also asked Dick Dorworth, the assistant men's coach working with the racers in the United States, to remove him from the team as soon as possible. Dorworth was alleged to have countered by saying that Shanny was too good a skier to lose and that he himself would quit the team if Shanny were dropped.

"There has been a direct personality clash between Willy and Shanholtzer all season," said Dorworth. "Willy is trying, successfully, to railroad Shanny off the team." Then Dorworth resigned, with no notice to Willy or the U.S.S.A., and went mountain climbing.

"There is no personality clash and I'm not trying to get rid of Shanholtzer," said Willy. The dispute and rumors had a damaging effect on Willy, Shanny and the team. It became apparent to the ski politicians that there was unrest, and some factions looked at the dispute as a way to remove Willy from his job. The team was bewildered. One or the other, Willy or Shanny, was resorting to subterfuge. The dispute, which had not yet developed into a person-to-person confrontation between Shanny and Willy, such as Tyler had had, did not improve his confidence. He finished poorly.

"I was in the starting gate, and all of a sudden the thought occurred to me—what if they cancel my ticket home—how will I get back?" Shanny had started the season with a total fortune of two hundred dollars, and had about ninety dollars left. But Shanny was more concerned about his liberty. "I'm just fed up with Willy's inflexible attitude. He's under the illusion we are skiing for him, and he worries about how he looks in the States. Not wearing jeans to dinner and having short hair isn't going to make us race better. Willy's trying to convey a team image of clean-cut American youth. He does not realize that the people who contribute the money are not the people who are spending an important time of their lives and a lot of effort and frustration busting their ass racing and, in my case, in downhill, so to speak risking their lives. We're not racing for those people, we're racing for ourselves. When you spend that much time, risk so much, put so much into it, dammit, you should do it a little more your own way.

"I learned a lot this winter, though, and I wouldn't have missed it. It's really neat about Tyler, that he got it, when it's so hard to get, and he kept it when it is so hard to keep. Because they've done everything to take it away from him." In the giant slalom at Sugarloaf, Shanny came in last.

While the American racers and coaches were trying to find themselves, worrying about finances, complaining about the U.S.S.A., resenting authority and discipline, the European hotshots were concentrating on winning races and the World Cup. The circuit was two-thirds completed and three racers, the Frenchmen Henri Duvillard and Patrick Russel, and the young Italian, Gustavo Thoeni, were within seconds of each other. World Cup points in 1971 were computed on the racers' three best finishes in each event—slalom, giant slalom and downhill. A first place was worth 25 points, second was 20, third was 15, fourth was 11. Points were scaled down until tenth position, which was valued at one World Cup point. The system was organized in this fashion so that the skier who excelled in the three events could gather the largest number of points. There have been very few skiers who are "polyvalent," who excel in all three events. Toni Sailer, now putting on weight in Kitzbühel, was one of this century's super skiers and proved it by winning three gold medals in the 1956 Olympics. Jean-Claude Killy pulled the same stunt in the 1968 Olympics. In 1967, the first year the World Cup was held, he became the first and only skier to score the maximum in the World Cup points—nine firsts, three in each event, for a perfect score of 225 points. The only skier at Sugarloaf who had come close was Karl Schranz, but at thirty-two he was losing his timing for slalom. The newcomers, for the most part, were specialists. The

Austrian Karl Cordin is a specialist in downhill as Tyler Palmer is in slalom. Augert is superb in slalom, good in giant slalom, nothing in downhill. Russel is a slalomist and giant slalomist, and poor in downhill. Thoeni has the same skills. Duvillard is a downhill specialist who is good in giant slalom and is developing into a slalomist. At Sugarloaf he was becoming the most versatile skier on the circuit. But as Duvillard developed in slalom, he seemed to be losing some of his downhill skill. Why? The coaches wondered. Was he losing this skill because he was progressing so quickly in slalom and giant slalom? Was the nervous, quick-reflexed skill of slalom and giant slalom overpowering the mental coolness and suppleness needed in downhill?

The development of a skier is unique. Karl Cordin was Austrian slalom champion when he was sixteen, then developed into a downhiller. Killy was first a slalomist and giant slalomist, then became a downhiller. Tyler Palmer expects to learn downhill now, after he has proven his ability in

Karl Schranz, two-time World Cup winner, realizes he is not going to make it this year.

slalom. "No one thinks I can do it, and I'd like to show them up." Tyler likes downhill and he says he will learn giant slalom last, as it is the most difficult. Giant slalom takes tremendous stamina and rhythm, and precise carved turns. Tyler figures it will take him at least three years to become a complete skier, and even then he is not sure whether he ever will become polyvalent.

At the beginning of the Sugarloaf race, Russel was in the lead, with 125 points, earned in slalom and giant slalom. Thoeni was close behind him, with 115 points earned in the same specialties. Duvillard had 105 points, earned in all three events. The odds were that Duvillard, with two downhills to run, would pull ahead.

From the beginning of his ski racing career, Thoeni had wanted to be a downhiller. Yet his inclination, and for that matter the skills of most young skiers, turned him to slalom. Thoeni has more natural ability than most skiers and at nineteen is a strong threat to Duvillard, twenty-three, and Russel, twenty-four, who are reaching the peak of their skill. Thoeni has light grey eyes and an easy smile. There is little sign of the worry, sternness, or maturity that mark the faces of most ski racers. Thoeni looks like a choir boy. He is quiet and reserved. He was born at home, in Trafio, Italy, a small mountain village a few kilometers from the Swiss border. The doctor had to ski in shortly after an avalanche had closed the road. He has been known as the child of snow, and his father, a ski instructor and climber, stated proudly that he had Gustavo skiing on the Stelvio glacier before he could walk. By the time Gustavo was eighteen, he was on the National A Team and was developing into an Italian hero. His nicknames are "L'angelo dello Stelvio" and "Il Killy italiano." He speaks Italian and German and is rapidly learning English.

Thoeni lives for skiing, simple and plain.

"What is your goal?"

"My goal is to win the World Cup."

"What do you think of in the morning?"

"Skiing."

"What do you do in the evenings?"

"I go to bed."

"Do you go out with girls?"

"I don't have time. I'm too young."

"What do you do in the summer?"

"I play tennis, swim, ski on glaciers. I am a Customs man, but I don't do much. I spend most of my time skiing."

"Why do you ski race?"

"Ski racing is beautiful."

Jean Vuarnet is the coach of the Italian team. He is very lucid, very intelligent. He noticed that Thoeni's left side was physically underdeveloped, perhaps from continually running slalom on a side hill at his home town, and Vuarnet worked on making it stronger. He did not push Thoeni into downhill, but let him develop as his talent and interest grew.

Vuarnet understood the downhill course at Sugarloaf perfectly. The last S turn—before a long flat that ended at the finish—was crucial. Most racers took a tight line, running the gate closely so they would hold their speed over the flat to the finish. Vuarnet instructed the Italians not to take the gate tightly, but to ride it high, to gain a little speed by skiing across the hill above the gate, then turn where the slope was high and use the extra height to press their skis over a small bump before the gate. They were to accelerate quickly where most racers would be riding their skis.

In the first downhill, Duvillard had placed second, behind the Swiss ace Russi. He hoped to win in the next downhill, picking up points over Thoeni and Russel because of their poor ability in downhill.

But the second downhill did not run as expected. Duvillard placed sixth, a poor finish for him, and picked up no additional World Cup points. The Italians, though, following their coach's advice, upset the hopes of the Austrians and Swiss. Stefano Anzi, the Italians' best downhiller, the one who pulled Rudd Pyles off the course when he was injured in December, flicked through the finish with the best time. Thoeni followed in the second seed. He could not believe it when his teammates started thumping him and the press and TV cameramen hard-shouldered their way to interview him and catch his image on film. He had finished third, the first time in his career that he had broken into the winner's circle in downhill. That happy, angelic smile lit his face and his grey eyes were shining. At first, he did not seem to comprehend what this unexpected victory meant. Then he realized he had picked up fifteen World Cup points and that he had forged ahead of Duvillard and Russel. The surprising victory was a boost to the young Italian's confidence, and he looked forward to winning in downhill.

Giant slalom is the offspring between downhill and slalom. The gates are open, as in downhill, and set on the hill so that the skier swings back and forth across the slope as he goes through them. It is a very rhythmical race, run faster than slalom. The turns are longer in radius, and each turn is linked. It is the most graceful of the three Alpine disciplines. It requires high technical ability to control the turns, and much strength.

Thoeni rides a very flat ski, with economy of motion. He skis close to the snow, and appears slow, but it is an illusion. He has won some races by a second and a half. The last race at Sugarloaf was two courses run on separate days. It was delayed when the truck van filled with the Swiss team's skis blew up and burned. No one was hurt but the Swiss had to borrow skis from other competitors. On the first run, after a snowfall, Thoeni glided through the course and won, closely followed by Duvillard. The second run Thoeni again had the best time, and Duvillard trailed in third place. Thoeni had put together a third and a first at Sugarloaf. Patrick Russel, who had been disqualified in the giant slalom, gave Thoeni a quick handshake and, smileless, turned around and disappeared in the crowd. Russel

With a mixture of happiness and disbelief, Gustavo Thoeni hears he has placed third in the downhill.

Henri Duvillard also hears the news of Thoeni's position.

Ann-Marie Proëll after she has taken the lead in the World Cup.

Michèle Jacot after she lost the lead in the World Cup.

had won no additional points at Sugarloaf. When they left the area for the next race in California, Thoeni was in the lead at 140 points and Duvillard and Russel remained at 125. It was that one race in downhill.

Thoeni was not the only victor who was riding high. Eighteen-year-old Anne-Marie Proëll is a young Austrian girl with freckles around her nose and a rosy complexion. She has the appearance of a healthy, hefty farm girl who milks the cows, which is what she was before she started ski racing. At Sugarloaf, she finished first in the two downhills and took away the World Cup lead from the French star, Michèle Jacot.

Silver axes were given to the winners. Although the French were far ahead as a team in aggregate Nations Cup points, they were being thwarted by the Italian and Austrian teen-agers in their bid for an individual World Cup. At the beginning of the season, they had hoped, and expected, to win two World Cups. Now they were worried. Willy Schaeffler had nothing to worry about with his team. Tyler Palmer, the best American, had fifty-six World Cup points and trailed Thoeni by seventy-four. The American men's team was running sixth, behind France, Switzerland, Austria, Italy and Germany. There was some solace with the women's team; they were in third place behind France and Austria.

First there were the Indians, then the explorers, then the settlers. Then there were no Indians, and along came the gamblers, a new type of explorer. They settled on the Nevada side of Lake Tahoe, an Indian word, which, if you have faith in Mark Twain, means grasshopper soup. Some people take a dash of salt with Mark Twain and say Tahoe means "much water." Hardly anybody cares. They come to South Lake Tahoe, on the California-Nevada border, and they traipse onto the Nevada side, to the flashing neon effervescence of Harrah's, Harvey's, Barney's and the Sahara Tahoe. Morning, noon and night they are there at the gaming tables, playing, losing, winning, losing—blackjack, roulette, craps, $25,000-keno, slots and bingo. There are night shows with big names—Sammy Davis, Jr., Lawrence Welk, Dean Martin, Liberace. The huge casinos served sumptuous buffets of roast beef and chickpeas. It is luscious, this scene, but gener-

13. The Mausoleum

ally sterile. There are very few chairs to relax in, except at the gambling tables. The atmosphere is nonsexual; gambling juices seem to bring out an entirely different fever.

South Lake Tahoe, and the gambling area which is actually called Stateline, is one big revolving wheel of a modern, country-type America filled with the same people that rushed through the region to Sutter's Mill in search of the mother lode. The search is still on. It is one of the charms of America's American. Those three cherries might line up, a winning streak at blackjack. Bingo! Eternal Optimism, trying to make an easy buck.

Above the neon strip, past the signs selling real estate, past the motels with low rates and free coffee, pizzas, hot dogs, hamburgers, drugs, gas, extravagant shows, nightly buffets, dealers' breakfasts, is Heavenly Valley ski

Some Bonne Bell gals check out their supply of Amyl para-Dimethylamin-benzoate.

resort. They were sponsoring two slaloms and giant slaloms for the World Cup competitors. The American team felt at home, living in a motel, eating hamburgers with ketchup and drinking Cokes that did not have that acidy, stringent taste that they have in Europe. The Europeans were happy too. The ski resort gave them free hats, there was a free buffet at Harrah's, a cocktail and buffet at Heavenly Valley, where Governor Reagan's daughter sang off-key, and, if you had some money, there were all those gambling casinos.

Karl Schranz, last year's hero, was holding his own at the blackjack table, the Europeans' favorite game. They know from the casinos at Chamonix, Kitzbühel and Badgastein that the odds on blackjack are more favorable to the player than the odds on roulette. All the racers were in South Lake Tahoe, 2,000 miles from the rigors of Maine, where everything closes up tight at midnight, booze is hidden on Sunday, and gambling is an illegal sin.

Thoeni celebrated his twentieth birthday in Lake Tahoe, at a party sponsored by Spalding (remember? they own the company that makes the skis that Thoeni races on). It was hostessed by the western branch of the Bonne Bell Barbie Dolls, who with their cosmetic smiles passed out yoyos, jacks, bubble makers and paper airplanes, the proper goodies for a child prodigy's birthday party. Gustavo was living on a high that had started on

The Heavenly Valley slalom course above Lake Tahoe.

Gustavo Thoeni on his way to victory in the slalom.

Patrick Russel looked on in disbelief as Thoeni also won the giant slalom.

the downhill course in Maine, and he was skiing like a Vatican miracle; he had just won the slalom and giant slalom and the Governor's Cup. Russel was walking through the casinos, his hands tucked tight in his pockets, scowling. He had won no World Cup points at Heavenly Valley. Duvillard was still pushing, but Thoeni had increased his lead to eighteen points. It would be difficult for Duvillard to make it up, but he could. He is a rugged competitor. The American men had suffered ten disqualifications in the two races, but Tyler had, as he wanted, finished in the top three in slalom.

"You know, she skis just like Thoeni—very low close to the snow, fluid." Stein Eriksen was commenting on the style of Barbara Ann Cochran as she flicked through the slalom course. Barbara Ann went on to pull a Thoeni at Heavenly Valley—she won both the slalom and giant slalom.

Barbara Ann Cochran is all smiles after her double victory.

Her older sister Marilyn again caught a ski tip in the second run of the slalom and skied off the course sobbing. Better days were ahead.

Barbara Ann is short, pint-sized and cute. She has long blond hair and light hazel eyes. She smiles, giggles and blushes, particularly when she is with Rick Chaffee. She is usually quiet with strangers and prefers to let Marilyn do all the talking when they are together. Barbara Ann likes to ride horses during the summer and to water ski. But hidden under her shy, easygoing ways are a few other traits—aggressiveness, determination and a temper that rarely is released. It was released that day in Val d'Isère when she blasted Hank Tauber because she felt he was forcing her to train on a poor slope. Later she apologized. Barbara Ann had also been worried about money in Europe. She had attended school the previous summer, studying French, and had paid for the course with one hundred dollars her grandmother had given her. Then, when she had to fly from Vermont to California for a National Ski Team training session, she expected the U.S.S.A. to pay for the trip. They never did. In Europe, she did not have enough money to buy Christmas presents for her sisters and brothers, and this depressed her. So did the American press. "At Val d'Isère I saw a clipping that said Marilyn and I were expected to be the top racers and we could only manage a fifth." She, like the rest of the skiing Cochrans, would prefer to have her father for a coach because she believes, and perhaps rightly so, that he knows more about the technique of ski racing than any other coach in the United States, and he understands his children very well.

At Heavenly Valley she had a few dollars to her name, her sister Marilyn fifty cents. Barbara Ann decided not to attend the races still scheduled in Italy, France and Sweden. "I'm tired of Europe, and all that stuff; I want to race at home and have some fun. Even if I won over there, I still would not have a chance for the World Cup."

Betsy Clifford had stated in December, after she won the first slalom of the year, that she expected to win the World Cup. But on January 10, on the eve of a race in Switzerland, Betsy suddenly had flown home to Canada and stated to the press, "I may . . . announce my retirement."

Rumors flew, Betsy had had a nervous breakdown. The death of her brother, the result of an accident in a dune buggy, was deeply depressing. She was unnerved by the downhills. She had trouble with her coach, who

The bottom of the slalom hill at Heavenly Valley.

expected Betsy to train hard and follow an austere schedule. Betsy, accompanied by her mother, was back in Europe a week later, in time for a slalom in Austria, which she won. She concentrated on her slalom, finished second to Barbara Ann, smiling happily for the cameras in her red jump suit. She ended the season tied for first place in slalom with the pretty French racer Britt Lafforgue, and she no longer talked about winning the World Cup and Olympic gold medals. She was following closely the example of her fellow Canadian, Nancy Greene, who won the World Cup in '68–'69. But Betsy, too intense, first had to learn to control her aggressiveness.

Tyler Palmer, although also broke, was keen to be at the last men's race of the season, in Sweden. He was not happy, neither was he sad, with his third-place finish in the slaloms. "Well," he said when he heard the time, "I screwed up the first run pretty bad." Then he looked over the crowd. "Some good-looking chicks here, huh?" and he flashed a smile. A U.S.S.A. official approached him after a press interview. "Well," exclaimed the official, eyeing Tyler's rather dirty white team sweater, "I guess you don't have time to clean your sweater over there in Europe."

"No, man!" snapped Tyler. "It's that I don't have the bread." Tyler's brother Terry, the one who captured the ski establishment's press coverage because he was winning races in a Canadian-American version of the World Cup, finished twenty-fifth, his best finish in six races against the Europeans.

Across the very blue Lake Tahoe, and into the mountains, about an hour's drive from Heavenly Valley, is Squaw Valley. Just before the entrance to the ski area is what appears to be a green and white highway sign that announces, "Poulsen, Population 12. Elevation 6,200 feet." It is the home of Eric and his sister Sandy, their brothers, a niece, their parents, Wayne and Sandy, and a dog. Rick Chaffee, Eric and Sandy spent their nights here during the race. Young Sandy was eighteen and developing into one of the better racers on the girls' squad. In the course of her career, she has broken her leg seven times. All of them had raced well at Heavenly—Eric had finished fifth in the giant slalom, Rick sixth in slalom, and they were feeling at home. It was the first time this year any of them had been in a home and it was a welcome respite from the sterility of hotel and motel bedrooms and repetitive communal feedings. They could sit at the large dining table and talk or relax in a sofa by the fire and read American magazines and newspapers. There was good skiing on the mountain, and it was a warm feeling to be home, with parents, to relax in privacy and not feel on display. And it was a good feeling for Eric to be in familiar surroundings, where he hunts and fishes in the summer and fall. Trophies from hunts Eric and his father and brothers have been on and medals from their skiing successes filled the hallway and game room.

Eric Poulsen is the best giant slalomist on the American team, and he is, so to speak, the highest bred race horse. He is very nervous before a race. Around his right knee he wears a leather strap. Never touch it—it is for good luck. He cannot stop moving, sliding his skis back and forth in the confined space where the racers wait near the starting gate. Eric needs someone to talk to him all the time. Once Hanspeter was busy with another racer and Eric pulled him over. "Why don't you talk to me?" Hanspeter usually does, soothingly, to cool down Eric's nervousness. It works, slightly, until the countdown, and then Eric explodes out of the gate. In one race he knocked down the timing device, and sometimes he forgets to jump forward in the starting gate and instead jumps up in the air, lands, then pushes himself out of the gate. Eric needs to run the first two gates well or he will not find his rhythm and will not race well.

"Now, Eric," said Hanspeter before the slalom in St.-Moritz, "the second gate is rutted. If you lean into it too much, your bindings and boots will hit the rut and knock you off balance. Don't lean in on this gate!"

"Okay," mumbled Eric. He was champing at the bit. He flew out of the starting gate and hit the second gate on the course. He had leaned in too much, his bindings and boots hit the inside of the rut, and he fell. Hanspeter quietly watched the spill from the starting gate. He was probably swearing to himself in German.

Eric, nineteen, looks like a chipmunk when he smiles. He is quiet, serious about racing, and polite; he once apologized to Hanspeter for not running a good race. He has active dreams. In training at Aspen, Eric, sound asleep, got out of bed and dragged all the shoes and boots in the dorm—tennis shoes, running shoes, loafers, ski boots, afterski boots—and placed them on his bed. Then he crawled under the pile and went back to sleep. In the morning when he awoke, he was amazed to find himself buried in bed with everyone's footwear.

In the Kandahar race at Crans-Montana, Switzerland, Eric had his best finish, fourth. After the race, Hanspeter and Michel Arpin compared the halfway times, and when Eric walked into the hotel lobby, where they were sitting, Hanspeter congratulated him, mentioning that he had the fastest time on the top of the course, "You're getting there, Eric."

Eric blinked a few times and stared at Hanspeter. Then, without saying anything, he turned and walked toward the door of the hotel. The shoulder muscles under his coat were tense and he hit his hand in his fist. "Yeah," he said softly, "I'm getting there."

Eric's father Wayne is a Pan Am pilot who in college was a four-event ski champion. He began purchasing property in Squaw Valley in the late thirties and developed Squaw Valley ski resort. He lost it in a hassle with Alex Cushing, who became president of the corporation and brought the 1960 Winter Olympics to the valley. The Poulsens now own only a couple of thousand acres at Squaw, and the ski resort, which has some of the best open slope skiing in America, is falling into disrepair. All the Poulsen children cut their teeth on a steep mountain called KT 22, where their father coached them. Their mother, a beautiful woman, is also a race enthusiast. She and her husband visited the first two races in Europe and helped the coaches with small details. Mrs. Poulsen learned a lot. "Our California kids have no chance to cut their teeth in Europe as the Europeans do. Safety is too important here. We mollycoddle them in the U.S." She was also surprised at some of the foreign skiers' appearances. "Our kids are ambassadors and it depends upon goodwill to raise money. Augert and Russel—their hair is long enough to braid!" She appreciates the fact that Eric is so quiet that few of the press ever bother to interview him and he does not get into any controversy. "The circuit is a ratrace," she continued, "and the politics indirectly affect our racers. I hope we get some sort of continuity."

Eric and Sandy Poulsen hoped to bring back to Squaw Valley Olympic medals won in Japan. They grew up under the glamor of the 1960 Olympics held in their front yard. It was the biggest ski event ever staged in the United States and it was also the first one to be televised. It turned many Americans on to the sport of skiing. That was eleven years ago, when Eric was eight and was racing in a junior league.

As Eric and Sandy grew into young teen-agers, the site of the Olympics,

Eric Poulsen in the starting gate. He is the most nervously charged of the American racers.

their home town, slowly deteriorated. Squaw Valley became practically a deserted village during the week nights. In the Squaw Valley Lodge cocktail lounge a pasty-faced bartender ignored customers and talked with his friends. He served drinks sullenly. Downstairs in the same lodge was a poster, tacked onto the stairway wall, that shouted the delights of summer in Squaw Valley. "Yes," it read, "the glories of Squaw Valley without all that damp snow . . . Vistas unmarred by dreadful glare—Athaletics [that was the way they spelled it] at 6,000 feet . . . Swimming and riding and other sensual sports . . . The vices of Reno . . . And now you can do it all barefoot . . . We will take care of your wife while you are off killing . . ." One of the events scheduled for the summer was a tournament of dominoes. The Poulsens never visit the Squaw Valley Lodge, they just ski the slopes.

Directly across from the Poulsen home is the Olympic Ice-Skating Rink. Snow had drifted onto some of the seats and the younger crowd were playing broomball. The scoreboard had not been changed since America beat Russia in that unexpected hockey upset eleven years earlier. Over the entrance to the rink hung the flags of the competing nations, and inside the building were stored the papier-maché statues of a ski jumper, a hockey player, a female figure skater and an Alpine skier. The statues have had holes punched into them, and are a dirty, grey color.

Over it all, staring down on this mausoleum, was a caricature of the American eagle, very ferocious looking, perhaps designed by one of the California Birchers. On plaques hung on a wall were listed the names of the winners—Jean Vuarnet, first, downhill. He is now the Italian team coach, and his name was spelled incorrectly. There were others, the American victors Penny Pitou and Betsy Snite, names from the past, their victories inscribed in obscure record books, rarely ever looked at, forgotten accomplishments except in the shadows of their mind—a ski-racing victory is a very personal event.

Outside, a gusty wind rattled a beer can across the empty, dark parking lot, until it landed in a snowbank. The week before, a chair had fallen off one of the lifts.

Perhaps the Poulsens' names would someday be inscribed on plaques, and their accomplishment a memory, but during the few days they rested at Squaw they dismissed ski racing from their minds and skied the deep powder on KT 22. It was the best fun of the season. Then Eric, Rick, and

Sandy packed their bags, said good-bye to the senior Poulsens and with the other racers, all those who hoped secretly and not so secretly to win an Olympic medal, vacated California, just as other racers had eleven years earlier. There were other places to go, and the last race of the World Cup circuit was in Åre, Sweden, 6,000 miles to the northeast.

There is a story that Rip McManus, a well-known ex-racer, tells about a conversation he had with some European coaches and racers when he was competing on the American team in the mid-sixties. The American racers, then as now, were not producing many victories, and the Europeans were razzing Rip about the poor quality of the American skiers and their ski program. Rip would not take it. "Just you wait!" he said, shaking his finger at them. "We have a secret team that has been training for the past year in Alaska and when they come over, they'll beat the pants off you! And you know what? They're all Negroes!"

The Europeans went bugeyed, their faces paled. They gasped, and one coach choked on his beer. They were sure it was no joke. "When are you bringing them over?" a coach whispered. Rip broke up.

The Europeans have a healthy respect for the black American athlete.

14. The Survivors

This group of professionals actually seemed to believe that if the Americans fielded an all-black national ski team, they would shortly be winning most of the ski races. How come? Some might say that the American black is superior in physique and conditioning. Yet many whites have the same abilities. More likely it comes down to a psychological factor that the black Americans share with the European racer. Motivation.

You take a basketball coach, give him a gym and $225,410, which was the Alpine program budget of the U.S.S.A. over the current year, and set him down in Philadelphia and tell him to field a team. How do you think he would do? He would be swamped, mostly with black athletes. His main problem as coach would be to winnow down the applicants to the best athletes. There would be no problem with motivation, for they would realize that competition in sport is a chance to win and a chance for a better life.

The U.S. Ski Team worried Willy Schaeffler. For the most part, they lacked strong motivation. How do you motivate a white, teen-aged kid, brought up near the American ski resorts, who, if he does not have what he wants, knows that it is easy enough, one way or another, sooner or later, to attain it?

The quest for the cup, a trip that would take the racers 30,000 miles in three months and a week, was ending in Åre, a small Swedish resort about 225 miles south of the Arctic circle. There would be held the last three races of the forty-seven-event circuit.

Patrick Russel, the dark, bushy-haired French ace, had expected to win the World Cup, but his numerous disqualifications in slalom and Thoeni's unexpected victory in the downhill had stolen his hope for victory. Karl Schranz, who the previous season had won the World Cup by three points over Russel, had given up early in the season, when he slightly injured his foot at St.-Moritz. He goofed through the rest of the season. In December, the ski press had picked him to win the World Cup. Among the women racers Michèle Jacot, the petite, sharp-featured French ace, had been expected to breeze to the cup, but as the last leg of the season progressed toward Åre, the farmer's daughter Anne-Marie Proëll eclipsed her hopes by winning two giant slaloms in Italy. Anne-Marie had earned the World Cup even before she boarded the plane to Åre, where she would again place first. Only Duvillard and Thoeni came into Åre with edginess in their gut; there was still a slight chance for Duvillard to snatch victory from Thoeni. But for the most part, the racers were subdued, resting in their rooms like so many short-term soldiers, waiting for that goal, which they had hoped to attain, to be won by someone else and put behind them, and their self-imposed prison to be ended.

The American team had been cut for this last trip, and only the successful veterans—Palmer, Chaffee, Poulsen and Kashiwa—were selected by their coaches for the trip. Hanspeter was with the team; Willy remained in Denver. There were four women, including Marilyn Cochran, who had just won the French National Championship, a free trip to the United States on the steamship *Le France,* and a Mickey Mouse watch from her coach, Hank Tauber. Marilyn was happy to go, for her boyfriend Henri Bréchu would also be in Åre.

Åre is in appearance similar to Sugarloaf, Maine. The mountain is

Gustavo Thoeni on his way to the World Cup
victory in Åre, Sweden.

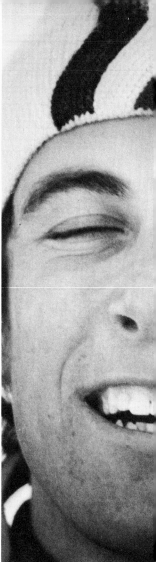

about the same size and there is a lake nearby that could be seen from the racers' rooms in the Tott Hotel. During the day ice fishermen basked in the sun and hoped to catch a few trout. Cross-country skiers flowed across the expanse and an occasional snowmobile scurried over the lake. The Swedish cherish their winters and for the first race of the series, a giant slalom, they trudged up the slope, carrying animal skins of reindeer, goat, even wolf, which they spread over the snow so they could sit with comfort, eat their lunch, and watch the activity. They, like the New Englanders,

Thoeni breaks up in happiness after his win.

have untanned complexions. But there is a tint of color, a bit more richness to their faces, perhaps because they are outside more, fishing or skiing cross country, or perhaps because they eat sardines, fishcakes, pickles, vegetable salads, pâté, salami, hard-boiled eggs, Wheaties and oatmeal for breakfast. At the races they snacked on hot dogs and french fries. Nearly everyone spoke English and the Americans felt very much at home.

The winning of the World Cup was anticlimactic, the result of a freak accident. Halfway down the course, Duvillard bumped a control gate, the pole caught under his arm and the flag covered his face. He lost vision for a moment, missed the next control gate and was disqualified. He skied down through the course, through the pine trees to the finish where waited the reporters, photographers, autograph-seeking children, and the officials. He snapped off his skis, looked toward the lake and shrugged. He had lost. Thoeni, skiing gracefully, relaxed down the course and finished fifth. His teammates jubilantly hoisted him to their shoulders as the press jostled forward and the young autograph collectors scurried into the fray. It was Italy's first World Cup. A few hours later, at a press conference, Thoeni mentioned that he had felt he would win if he did well in a downhill. After his third place in Maine, he was sure of carrying out the prediction he had made in December at the beginning of the season, that he would win the World Cup. Most of the press, and the racers, had thought this a brash statement coming from a nineteen-year-old mountain boy starting his second winter in the World Cup circuit.

"And what does winning the World Cup mean to you?" asked a Swedish journalist. A very happy Italian journalist stood up and faced the press and with a big smile answered for Thoeni, "Sixty million lire!" The year before, Thoeni, according to the Italian press, had earned 40 million lire.

"Gosh," said Hank Kashiwa, lying in his bed in the Tott Hotel, "I got to work, or they'll put me in jail for not paying my bills." He had no job lined up and was concerned about the summer. He and Rick Chaffee were rooming together. Neither had done well in the race and they were trying to relax and forget. Rick had given Hank *Psycho-Cybernetics* to read, and Hank had given Rich *Everything You Always Wanted to Know about Sex.* Both of them were engrossed.

Tyler Palmer was in the next room with Eric Poulsen. Tyler had finished last in the giant slalom and was looking at the scoresheet upside down. "Looks a lot better that way, huh?" he grinned. The next day he would finish seventh in the slalom, poor for what he had set for himself, particularly since his chief competitor, Jean-Noël Augert, finished first, his fifth World Cup victory in a row.

Tyler was also worried about the summer. He was hoping to work in the Lange ski boot factory in Colorado, but he was not sure whether the U.S.S.A. would allow it. Before the season Tyler had taken the money he had earned in construction, three hundred dollars, and invested part of it in a car that his brother Terry used to travel the American ski circuit. He then gave Terry the rest of the cash for expenses.

The award ceremonies were a formal affair attended by Crown Prince Gustaf and took place a few hours after the slalom race, not in Åre but in Östersund, sixty kilometers distant. From there the racers would leave by air for their home countries.

A basketball court became the ceremony hall. On one side of the court, filling the bleachers, were several thousand residents of Östersund. On the opposite side, flanked by four buglers and two flag holders, the town band played solemn, regal music. Two sets of chairs opposed each other on the basketball court, where the racers would sit after filing in. In the center was a pedestal for the award winners to stand on and in front of that were two long tables filled with awards, including the World Cups. Crown Prince Gustaf would give the trophies and shake the hands of the winners. He is a young man, twenty-five, a ski enthusiast.

The band played solemnly and on cue the racers paraded from the gym room to the basketball court, alphabetically by country. A basketball bounced across the court, kicked by a playful racer, as they marched by columns of two—the Austrians, Finnish, French, Germans, Italians, Japanese, Norwegians, Poles, Spaniards, Swiss, Swedes, and, ill at ease with the military bearing of the moment, the Americans, led by Rick Chaffee and Marilyn Cochran. Tyler Palmer had a sheepish grin on his face.

As soon as they were seated, four young hostesses, dressed in long skirts that split in the middle to reveal white hot pants, placed a medal around each racer's neck. The prettiest hostess was enveloped in a tight embrace after she decorated one of the Spanish racers. The crowd began to giggle and loosen up. The pomp of having the Crown Prince present did not faze the skiers.

Thoeni, for his second place in the slalom in Åre, the last race of the season, received a portable typewriter, which he looked at with amazement as he shook Prince Gustaf's hand. He did not know how to type. Augert won a bicycle and, with that wild grin of his, rode it from the pedestal around the gym to the accompaniment of the band, then took another turn with Duvillard riding on the back. Even the Prince was amused.

Tyler wore a long-sleeved wine-colored shirt with little flowers on it, which appeared to match his hair. He blushed deeply when the Prince gave him his medal, and he loped back to his seat. He had ended the sea-

The winners, Italy's Gustavo Thoeni, a mountain boy, and Austria's Ann-Marie Proëll, a farmer's daughter.

son as the third best slalomist in the world and the tenth best skier in the World Cup. The season before he had been rated seventy-third.

The glass globes, the World Cups, were presented to Anne-Marie Proëll, who flushed with embarrassment, and Gustavo Thoeni, who skipped up to receive his cup, a cool smile on his face. The photographers snapped away and then the two World Cup champions handed the trophies back to an official, who placed them in separate leather containers. The official presentation would be made six weeks later, at another formal affair in Evian, France, the home town of the mineral water people. In the meantime, the Evian representative was making sure the cups would not be broken.

The French were presented with the Nations Cup—sponsored by America's *Ski* Magazine—for having the best men's and women's team, and the ceremony, with a ruffle and flourish, was over. The racers marched out, except for Augert and Duvillard, who double-teamed it on the new bike. The American team had finished fourth, behind the French, Austrian, and Swiss. If it had not been for the women's victories they would have finished sixth.

The award ceremony was followed by a banquet of steak, potatoes, beans and large flasks of red wine. Hank Kashiwa and Tyler Palmer had taken some roses from the table decoration and hung them from their ears; they were becoming very happy with the wine. A rock band roared and everyone bounced on the dance floor. Rick Chaffee danced with his arms extended, the same way he runs slalom. Thoeni was at last devoting some attention to girls, and he was rocking smoothly with a minimum of motion. Palmer did a lot of angulating. The skiers' dance techniques seemed to reflect their ski techniques, and one wondered . . . One of the hostesses, a tall and strikingly beautiful blonde, danced the slow numbers with Hanspeter. She could not seem to take her hands off him. Contrary to rumors, not all Swedish women are blond and beautiful. There are also brunettes, and both colors come in packages of many different shapes and sizes. But it is true that there are many tall, very attractive girls and they do not fool. If they like you, you know it very quickly. And if they do not dig you, you learn that quickly too.

But most of the racers had little time to remain in Östersund and play with the charming girls. There was a chartered flight to catch and the nightclub emptied quickly. Thoeni skipped out of the club, his eyes dancing. Hanspeter, all blushes, was fighting off the young Swedish hostess, who broke into tears after he backed out the door. Tyler, in a rollicking mood, with a glass of wine, gave a roaring send-off to his friend Jean-Noël and his buddy Dudu. The Frenchmen then retrieved their bicycle from the cloakroom, wheeled it out the front door and, wobbling dangerously, bicycled down the street, warmly lit by large glass bulbs, and disappeared around a corner. At the airport, they would find the ski bags of six teams jumbled into a two-ton mess. It took them two hours to find their equipment. The World Cup was over.

Two months later World Cup champion Gustavo Thoeni was promoted to corporal in the Italian Customs Services. The Cochrans visited President Nixon, who said "Thank you." Willy Schaeffler was in Colorado, looking for young racers with motivation.

Of the twenty-four men's races held between December 11 and March 14, the French won ten, the Swiss six, the Italians five, the Austrians two and the Americans, through Tyler Palmer, one. Of the twenty-three women's races, the French again won ten, the Austrians eight, the Americans, through the Cochrans, three and Canada's Betsy Clifford, two. For the Americans—four victories out of forty-seven races.

The Record Page

MEN *(cont.)*		
Special Slalom	*Points 1970–71*	*Position 1969–70*
1. Jean-Noël Augert, *France*	75	3
2. Gustavo Thoeni, *Italy*	70	4
3. Tyler Palmer, *USA*	60	not ranked
4. Patrick Russel, *France*	55	1
5. Harald Röffner, *Austria*	46	7
6. Christian Neureuther, *W. Germany*	41	19
7. Alain Penz, *France*	38	2
8. David Zwilling, *Austria*	33	24
9. Edmund Bruggmann, *Switzerland*	29	29
10. Rick Chaffee, *USA*	28	10
21. Hank Kashiwa, *USA*	6	39
29. Eric Poulsen, *USA*	2	30

Giant Slalom	*Points 1970–71*	*Position 1969–70*
1. Patrick Russel, *France* ⎫(Tie)	70	2
1. Gustavo Thoeni, *Italy* ⎭	70	1
3. Edmund Bruggmann, *Switzerland*	65	10
4. Henri Duvillard, *France*	60	17
5. David Zwilling, *Austria*	51	28
6. Sepp Heckelmiller, *W. Germany*	46	11
7. Jean-Noël Augert, *France*	32	6
8. Werner Bleiner, *Austria*	25	4
8. Christian Neureuther, *W. Germany*	25	21
8. Bernhard Russi, *Switzerland*	25	19
14. Eric Poulsen, *USA*	15	29
21. Rick Chaffee, *USA*	3	31

MEN *(cont.)*

Downhill	*Points 1970–71*	*Position 1969–70*
1. Bernhard Russi, *Switzerland*	70	5
2. Bernard Orcel, *France*	60	5
3. Karl Cordin, *Austria*	56	2
4. Henri Duvillard, *France*	53	3
5. Walter Tresch, *Switzerland*	46	not ranked
6. Jean-Daniel Daetwyler, *Switzerland*	44	10
7. Stefano Anzi, *Italy*	40	29
8. Karl Schranz, *Austria*	38	1
9. Andrea Sprecher, *Switzerland*	25	14
9. Franz Vogler, *W. Germany*	25	5
14. Craig Shanholtzer, *USA*	8	not ranked
23. Bob Cochran, *USA*	2	31
23. Hank Kashiwa, *USA*	2	not ranked
23. Mike Lafferty, *USA*	2	19

WOMEN

Combined	*Points 1970–71*	*Position 1969–70*
1. Anne-Marie Proëll, *Austria*	210	7
2. Michèle Jacot, *France*	177	1
3. Isabelle Mir, *France*	133	9
4. Wiltrud Drexel, *Austria*	124	16
5. Françoise Macchi, *France*	122	2
6. Britt Lafforgue, *France*	112	10
7. Jacqueline Rouvier, *France*	101	39
8. Barbara Ann Cochran, *USA*	90	5
9. Gertrud Gabl, *Austria*	87	17
10. Betsy Clifford, *Canada*	76	8
11. Marilyn Cochran, *USA*	74	14
17. Karen Budge, *USA*	34	15
22. Sandra Poulsen, *USA*	17	not ranked
24. Susie Corrock, *USA*	14	31
26. Patty Boydstun, *USA*	12	31
30. Rosie Fortna, *USA*	4	24

WOMEN *(cont.)*

Special Slalom	Points 1970–71	Position 1969–70
1. Britt Lafforgue, *France*	70	1
2. Betsy Clifford, *Canada*	70	4
3. Barbara Ann Cochran, *USA*	65	3
3. Anne-Marie Proëll, *Austria*	65	15
5. Michèle Jacot, *France*	56	2
6. Florence Steurer, *France*	51	8
7. Wiltrud Drexel, *Austria*	45	not ranked
8. Gertrud Gabl, *Austria*	37	16
8. Berni Rauter, *Austria*	37	4
10. Marilyn Cochran, *USA*	33	11
10. Danièle Debernard, *France*	33	not ranked
18. Patty Boydstun, *USA*	12	not ranked
22. Susie Corrock, *USA*	4	22
22. Rosie Fortna, *USA*	4	19

Giant Slalom	Points 1970–71	Position 1969–70
1. Anne-Marie Proëll, *Austria*	75	3
2. Michèle Jacot, *France*	70	1
3. Françoise Macchi, *France*	60	1
4. Gertrud Gabl, *Austria*	50	14
5. Isabelle Mir, *France*	48	not ranked
6. Britt Lafforgue, *France*	42	9
6. Jacqueline Rouvier, *France*	42	not ranked
8. Marilyn Cochran, *USA*	34	12
9. Rosi Mittermaier, *W. Germany*	29	11
10. Karen Budge, *USA*	28	10
12. Barbara Ann Cochran, *USA*	25	4
14. Sandra Poulsen, *USA*	17	not ranked
23. Susie Corrock, *USA*	3	not ranked

WOMEN (*cont.*)

Downhill	Points 1970–71	Position 1969–70
1. Anne-Marie Proëll, *Austria*	70	8
2. Wiltrud Drexel, *Austria*	60	6
3. Françoise Macchi, *France*	56	5
4. Isabelle Mir, *France*	55	1
4. Jacqueline Rouvier, *France*	55	21
6. Michèle Jacot, *France*	51	4
7. Annie Famose, *France*	29	2
8. Divina Galica, *Gr. Britain*	11	20
9. Margret Hafen, *W. Germany*	9	13
9. Florence Steurer, *France*	9	3
11. Marilyn Cochran, *USA*	7	16
11. Susie Corrock, *USA*	7	not ranked
13. Karen Budge, *USA*	6	13

NATIONS CUP

Combined	Points 1970–71	Position 1969–70
1. France	1,333	1
2. Austria	892	2
3. Switzerland	396	4
4. USA	373	3
5. West Germany	241	5
6. Italy	226	6
7. Canada	99	7
8. Spain	42	13
9. Poland	41	8
10. Great Britain	22	11

NATIONS CUP (*cont.*)

Men	*Points 1970–71*	*Position 1969–70*
1. France	505	1
2. Switzerland	388	3
3. Austria	361	2
4. Italy	223	4
5. West Germany	171	6
6. USA	128	5
7. Poland	41	7
8. Spain	15	12
9. Australia	7	8
10. Norway	4	11

Women	*Points 1970–71*	*Position 1969–70*
1. France	828	1
2. Austria	531	3
3. USA	245	2
4. Canada	97	4
5. West Germany	70	5
6. Spain	27	not ranked
7. Great Britain	22	7
8. Switzerland	8	6
9. Italy	3	9

Photo Credits

Evian Co.: *page 4*

Del Mulkey: *pages 14, 38, 41, 58, 68, 69, 72, 74, 124, 149*

Fred Lindholm: *page 79*

Photo Agence France-Presse: *page 221*

All other photographs are by Peter Miller

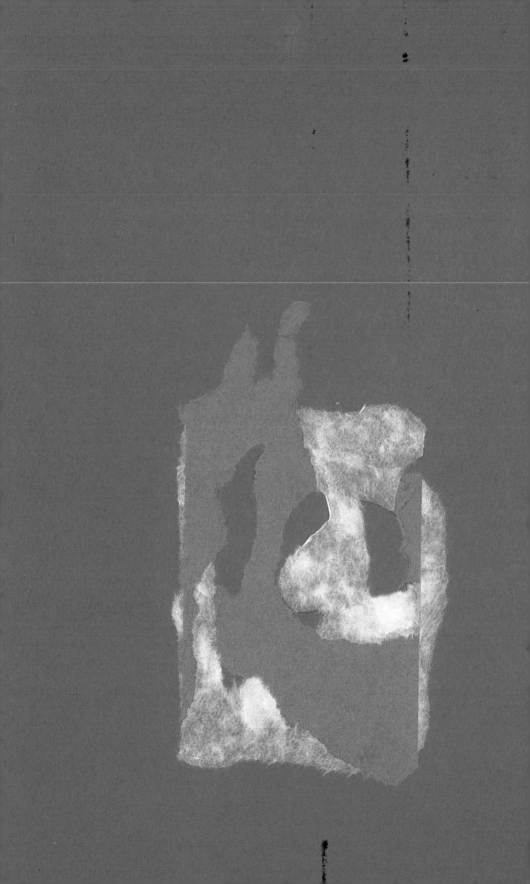